Lesbians, Levis and Lipstick:
The Meaning of Beauty
in Our Lives

Lesbians, Levis and Lipstick: The Meaning of Beauty in Our Lives
has been co-published simultaneously as *Journal of Lesbian Studies,*
Volume 3, Number 4 1999.

Lesbians, Levis and Lipstick: The Meaning of Beauty in Our Lives

Jeanine C. Cogan, PhD
Joanie M. Erickson
Editors

Lesbians, Levis and Lipstick: The Meaning of Beauty in Our Lives, edited by Jeanine C. Cogan and Joanie M. Erickson, was simultaneously issued by The Haworth Press, Inc., under the same title, as a special issue of *Journal of Lesbian Studies,* Volume 3, Number 4 1999, Esther D. Rothblum, Editor.

Harrington Park Press
An Imprint of
The Haworth Press, Inc.
New York • London • Oxford

ISBN 1-56023-121-1

Published by

Harrington Park Press, 10 Alice Street, Binghamton, NY 13904-1580 USA

Harrington Park Press is an imprint of The Haworth Press, Inc., 10 Alice Street, Binghamton, NY 13904-1580 USA.

Lesbians, Levis and Lipstick: The Meaning of Beauty in Our Lives has been co-published simultaneously as *Journal of Lesbian Studies* ™, Volume 3, Number 4 1999.

The development, preparation, and publication of this work has been undertaken with great care. However, the publisher, employees, editors, and agents of The Haworth Press and all imprints of The Haworth Press, Inc., including The Haworth Medical Press® and Pharmaceutical Products Press®, are not responsible for any errors contained herein or for consequences that may ensue from use of materials or information contained in this work. Opinions expressed by the author(s) are not necessarily those of The Haworth Press, Inc.

Library of Congress Cataloging-in-Publication Data

Lesbians, Levis and lipstick : the meaning of beauty in our lives / Jeanine C. Cogan, Joanie M. Erickson, editors.
     p. cm.
     Co-published simultaneously as Journal of lesbian studies, vol. 3, no. 4, 1999.
     Includes bibliographical references and index.
     ISBN 0-7890-0661-8 (alk. paper).–ISBN 1-56023-121-1 (alk. paper)
     1. Feminine beauty (Aesthetics) 2. Lesbians–Attitudes. 3. Beauty, Personal. I. Cogan, Jeanine C. II. Erickson, Joanie M. III. Journal of lesbian studies.
HQ1219.L476 1999
305.48'9664–dc21
                                                      99-31178
                                                      CIP

INDEXING & ABSTRACTING

Contributions to this publication are selectively indexed or abstracted in print, electronic, online, or CD-ROM version(s) of the reference tools and information services listed below. This list is current as of the copyright date of this publication. See the end of this section for additional notes.

- *Abstracts in Social Gerontology: Current Literature on Aging*

- *BUBL Information Service, an Internet-based Information Service for the UK higher education community*

- *CNPIEC Reference Guide: Chinese National Directory of Foreign Periodicals*

- *Contemporary Women's Issues*

- *Feminist Periodicals: A Current Listing of Contents*

- *Gay & Lesbian Abstracts*

- *GenderWatch*

- *HOMODOK/"Relevant" Bibliographic database, Documentation Centre for Gay & Lesbian Studies, University of Amsterdam (selective printed abstracts in "Homologie" and bibliographic computer databases covering cultural, historical, social and political aspects of gay & lesbian topics)*

- *Index to Periodical Articles Related to Law*

- *PAIS (Public Affairs Information Service) NYC*

- *Referativnyi Zhurnal (Abstracts Journal of the All-Russian Institute of Scientific and Technical Information)*

- *Sociological Abstracts (SA)*

- *Studies on Women Abstracts*

- *Women's Studies Index (indexed comprehensively)*

(continued)

*Special Bibliographic Notes related to special journal issues
(separates) and indexing/abstracting:*

- indexing/abstracting services in this list will also cover material in any "separate" that is co-published simultaneously with Haworth's special thematic journal issue or DocuSerial. Indexing/abstracting usually covers material at the article/chapter level.
- monographic co-editions are intended for either non-subscribers or libraries which intend to purchase a second copy for their circulating collections.
- monographic co-editions are reported to all jobbers/wholesalers/approval plans. The source journal is listed as the "series" to assist the prevention of duplicate purchasing in the same manner utilized for books-in-series.
- to facilitate user/access services all indexing/abstracting services are encouraged to utilize the co-indexing entry note indicated at the bottom of the first page of each article/chapter/contribution.
- this is intended to assist a library user of any reference tool (whether print, electronic, online, or CD-ROM) to locate the monographic version if the library has purchased this version but not a subscription to the source journal.
- individual articles/chapters in any Haworth publication are also available through the Haworth Document Delivery Service (HDDS).

ABOUT THE EDITORS

Jeanine C. Cogan, PhD, is a Congressional Science Fellow at the American Psychological Association in Washington, DC. Blending her expertise in public policy and as a social psychologist, she conducts research for and works to bring national attention to eating disorders and negative body image as a public health threat. Her research and public policy efforts have been recognized in articles appearing in the *Los Angeles Times*, *The Chicago Tribune*, and *The Houston Chronicle*. Serving as an educator in both the university and public settings, Dr. Cogan has conducted many presentations on the topic of women and beauty, with a recent emphasis on lesbian beauty. She has edited a recent journal issue entitled "Dying To Be Thin in the Name of Health" for the *Journal of Social Issues*.

Joanie M. Erickson is Director of Public Relations for a non-profit health care organization in Fairfield, California. Involved in the field of health care public relations for the last 15 years, Ms. Erickson has received many national awards, including the McEachern, given annually by the Public Relations Society of America, and the Touchstone from the American Hospital Association. She is also the former president of the Healthcare Public Relations & Marketing Society in California. In addition, Ms. Erickson enjoys writing poetry and short stories.

CONTENTS

Introduction

Jeanine C. Cogan
Joanie M. Erickson

IN SEARCH OF A DEFINITION

If you asked a group of lesbians if they find other lesbians beautiful, the answer would likely be a resounding "yes!"

By definition, lesbians find beauty in other women. But what is lesbian beauty? Jeanine, one of the co-editors of this publication, posed this question to a group of lesbians at a seminar. Their responses, woven throughout this introduction, indicate that lesbians have a broad definition of what makes a woman beautiful. This range of beauty, which emerges from the authors featured in this publication, as well as in our own reflections on lesbian beauty, is a stark contrast to the narrow dominant cultural definitions which are typically defined by physical aesthetics. As one woman at the seminar answered the question "What is lesbian beauty?":

> ... *strong women, laughter, a certain walk, a certain style, strong arms, strong legs, great earrings, honest, confident, indefinable yet I know what it is* ...

SHOOTING DOWN THE STEREOTYPES

Research shows that the dominant culture perceives lesbians as less attractive than straight women (Dew, 1985; Unger, Hilderbrand, & Madar, 1982). In the movie *Good Morning Vietnam*, the character played by Robin Williams

[Haworth co-indexing entry note]: "Introduction." Cogan, Jeanine C., and Joanie M. Erickson. Co-published simultaneously in *Journal of Lesbian Studies* (The Haworth Press, Inc.) Vol. 3, No. 4, 1999, pp. 1-9; and: *Lesbians, Levis and Lipstick: The Meaning of Beauty in Our Lives* (ed: Jeanine C. Cogan and Joanie M. Erickson) The Haworth Press, Inc., 1999, pp. 1-9; and: *Lesbians, Levis and Lipstick: The Meaning of Beauty in Our Lives* (ed: Jeanine C. Cogan and Joanie M. Erickson) Harrington Park Press, an imprint of The Haworth Press, Inc., 1999, pp. 1-9. Single or multiple copies of this article are available for a fee from The Haworth Document Delivery Service [1-800-342-9678, 9:00 a.m. - 5:00 p.m. (EST). E-mail address: getinfo@haworthpressinc.com].

1

defined a lesbian as a woman who wears comfortable shoes. We've all heard similar stereotypes about the physical appearance of lesbians: short hair, drab, dour, masculine dress, unappealing, unattractive, too ugly to find a man.

An old boyfriend once said to me 'all lesbians are short' . . .

Like all stereotypes, these are not an accurate representation. Drab, dour and unattractive we are not. Some of the world's most beautiful women are lesbians found at clubs and events, on movie and television screens, in magazines, and even in our own mirrors. We can toss the "too ugly to get a man" stereotype out with the flannel shirts. Yet, generalizations can be made about lesbians' styles. For instance, many lesbians (but not all) do cut their hair short, a subject that is discussed by a number of authors in this publication. Although no research has been conducted on the "comfortable shoes" phenomenon, few of us are likely to be found teetering about on three-inch heels. And, okay, many of us do have more tailored suit coats hanging in our closets than the "average" woman.

DO LESBIAN BEAUTY NORMS EXIST?

Lesbian beauty norms clearly are broader than traditional beauty norms, encompassing a wider range of sizes, shapes, ethnicity and styles. In working on this publication, we found a greater emphasis on what we call "holistic beauty."

Lesbian beauty for me is about confidence and self-acceptance. I can find a woman of any style, color, size and mix of feminine and masculine beautiful if she sends a signal that she is comfortable in her own skin. It's an attitude.

We scanned the personal ads in a Sacramento, California, alternative newspaper to explore the words lesbians used to describe what they seek in potential partners. Similar to the findings of the classic study by Deaux and Hanna (1984), we observed the traditional descriptions of desired physical aesthetics to be replaced with words like "confident," "vibrant," "warm," "natural" and "sincere." Holistic beauty encompasses all parts of a woman; her self-image, intelligence, humor and a capacity for empathy and love are as important to a lesbian's "look" as her physical attributes.

Yet, lesbians do have beauty norms surrounding clothing, hair and make-up. Joanie, the other co-editor, recently sat down with a group of lesbians at a party. As she stretched out her legs, clad in faded blue Levi 501 jeans adorned with a black leather belt, she placed her black leather shoed feet firmly on the ground and made a dismaying observation: The five lesbians perched around the coffee table accounted for five pairs of faded Levi 501s, five black leather belts and five pairs of black leather shoes.

BUILDING A BIGGER CAGE: IS BEAUTY OUR BEAST, TOO?

Like people all over the world, lesbians have a need to feel they belong in their culture and to identify others in their group. Since no inherent physical attribute exists that allows us to safely identify each other, we create them and lesbian beauty norms are born. Clearly, our beauty norms don't oppress women in the same ways as in the dominant culture where female beauty means facial features sculpted by a plastic surgeon and bodies that look like 13-year-old boys with very large breasts. Many feel a sense of freedom about our appearance when we come out as lesbians.

However, as we listen to the voices in this publication, we learn that lesbian beauty norms can be constraining and emotionally damaging, as well. We liken lesbian beauty standards to building a bigger cage. As lesbians, we have much more room to experiment with beauty than our straight sisters. That we celebrate. Yet, for lesbians who need more room to feel beauty, the bars of the lesbian beauty cage still come too soon. Many lesbians feel limited by the beauty standards we have created.

WHY THIS PUBLICATION, WHY NOW?

Jeanine developed the idea of writing on lesbian beauty and Joanie eagerly agreed to partner with her on the effort. We dove into this project for a combination of intellectual curiosity, and professional and personal motivations.

Intellectual Curiosity

Much valuable work has been published on dominant cultural beauty standards and their effect on women (e.g., see Cogan, 1999, for review). However, analysis of beauty and sexual orientation is, for the most part, absent (see Rothblum, 1994, for review). Consequently, we don't know much about how these standards affect lesbians specifically and if lesbians have developed their own beauty norms. Whereas this publication focuses on the experiences of lesbians, some of the articles explore the experiences of bisexual women. Unless specifically indicated by the article author, discussions of lesbian beauty cannot be assumed to reflect bisexual women. Their viewpoint is a unique one, and worthy of independent study.

We decided to work on this publication to learn more about ourselves and our culture and to create a new body of information about notions of beauty and how lesbians respond to them, as individuals and as a community.

Professional Motivations

Jeanine is a social psychologist whose major fields of study are the social construction of beauty and lesbian/gay issues. Creating this publication blends her two professional interests and gives her the opportunity to explore new professional territory.

Joanie is a health care public relations executive by trade. Creating this publication gives her the chance to write beyond the limits of press releases and advertising copy and help other writers develop their insights and creativity.

Personal Motivations

We have been great friends for years. In our many walks, talks, meals and car rides together, we have discussed every aspect of our lives, including our own struggles with the beauty beast. We have both negotiated the perils of conventional beauty mandates and triumphed over them. Yet, we arrived at the same place from strikingly different paths.

By all measures but her own, Jeanine fit the stringent dominant cultural beauty norms. She was thin and feminine–having started dieting at the age of 12–and though she didn't think so, she looked great in those too-short-to-be-comfortable dresses. As a result she received the reward of beauty promised by the dominant culture: male attention. But this reward did not come without a high price for her: feelings of objectification, doubts of her abilities, and an eating disorder. As chronicled through her two poems in this publication, Jeanine was able to conquer her body hatred by embracing feminist ideals and rejecting the conventional beauty norms that were suffocating her. By learning to love her own body, Jeanine discovered she could love other women's bodies, as well, and her coming out process began. Coming out offered her a sense of freedom from damaging beauty expectations and she was able to play with new expressions of style. As she says now:

> *I love playing with the "sport dyke" look. When I put on a baseball cap and a nylon parka, I walk out of the door feeling strong and incredibly free.*

Unlike Jeanine, Joanie was never thin and feminine. She is 5'9" and rarely below 200 lbs. Growing up, she knew that fat was a fatal flaw. Fat and beautiful were oxymorons, and she never felt she had the capacity, or permission, to be beautiful. So, she rarely tried, and when she did try to "dress up"–do her hair, wear make-up, or attempt any other conventional beauty rituals–she felt like she was dressed up for a costume party, looking as ridiculous as if she were going out into the world in big red shoes and a rubber nose. When Joanie came out as a lesbian, she also came out as a beautiful woman.

> *When a woman tells me I'm beautiful, I feel it. Now, I don't dress up to attempt beauty. I dress up because, damn, I look good!*

EMERGING THEMES

As submissions came into our mailboxes and computer terminals, themes emerged about body image, broad definitions of beauty, and some of the ways lesbians are freed and constrained by the beauty norms we create. This publication is divided into three sections reflecting these themes: (1) In the Eye of the Beholder: Identifying and Defining Lesbian Beauty Norms; (2) Freedoms and Constraints of Lesbian Beauty Norms; and (3) Compulsory Thinness: Are Lesbians Immune from the Barbie Mandate?

In the Eye of the Beholder: Identifying and Defining Lesbian Beauty Norms

This section explores how lesbians create their own beauty norms, and how these norms impact them. Carol Wuebker's poem "Yeah, You" is an eloquent introduction to the infinite definition of lesbian beauty, and discards conventional beauty norms as frivolous.

In "Beauty Mandates and the Appearance Obsession: Are Lesbian and Bisexual Women Better Off?" Anna Myers, Jennifer Taub, Jessica Morris and Esther Rothblum empirically illustrate how many women feel freed from conventional beauty standards after they come out, while others continue to feel pressure to conform. Further, they examine the restrictions of lesbian beauty norms.

Jennifer Taub, in the article "Bisexual Women and Beauty Norms: A Qualitative Examination," found that the gender of a woman's partner affects appearance practices. Her results showed that bisexual women partnering with a male were more likely to adopt traditional beauty norms, while those partnering with females were more likely to adopt lesbian beauty norms.

In "Lesbians Discuss Beauty and Aging" Kim Thompson interviews three lesbians age 55 and older who discuss their personal beauty journeys within the lesbian community and the dominant culture. They provide insight into how lesbian attitudes evolve throughout the aging process.

In "Beauty on the Borderland: On Being Black Lesbian and Beautiful," an article by Jennifer Lyle, Jeanell Jones and Gail Drakes, three women of color share their experiences and perspectives on lesbian beauty. Through their engaging dialogue, they examine the functions of beauty in their communities, attractiveness and its meanings for them as women, as black women, and as black lesbians/bisexuals.

In "Doing Beauty: Negotiating Lesbian Looks in Everyday Life," Tania Hammidi and Susan Kaiser examine the multiple ways lesbians "do" beauty, and how conflicting cultural messages and constructions influence this. By recognizing beauty as a process of negotiation, they suggest the role of beauty for lesbians is empowering.

Freedoms and Constraints of Lesbian Beauty Norms

In this section, six authors share their personal experiences with and research findings on conventional and lesbian beauty norms. Some discuss the freedom they feel about their appearance as lesbians. Others point out ways lesbian beauty norms, while less constraining than dominant cultural beauty standards, marginalize those lesbians who don't conform to them.

Joanie Erickson shares the celebrations and freedom she found when she came out as a lesbian in her article "Confessions of a Butch Straight Woman." She looks at her view on beauty when she lived as a straight woman to her newfound comfort as a lesbian exploring the feminine and masculine sides of herself through her appearance.

In her poem "Invisible Womon" Beth Daily-Wallach paints a picture of femme lesbian invisibility. Yet she recognizes that she might also overlook femmes "as she saves her glances for the dyke."

Jeanine Cogan's article "Lesbians Walk the Tightrope of Beauty: Thin Is In but Femme Is Out" addresses how lesbians are influenced by and respond to beauty constructions of dominant culture while they simultaneously redefine and create their own meaning of beauty within lesbian communities. She empirically examines how lesbians use beauty markers as a form of identification within lesbian communities.

Dvora Zipkin, a self-confessed "long-haired lesbian," further discusses the theme of femme invisibility by looking at the discrimination experienced by lesbians who grow their hair long. Through her own experiences and interviews with seven lesbians and bisexual women, she attributes the higher value placed on masculine attributes to internalized sexism in lesbian culture.

"Even My Hair Won't Grow Straight" by Ellen Samuels asks why lesbians "give up" what is traditionally considered sexy, such as long hair and lingerie. Through her internal conflict she leads us to question whether any woman can be completely free from the politics of beauty.

In "Beauty and the Butch" Bonnie Strickland shares a compelling personal struggle with traditional beauty as a prescription for gender identification. She explores the interconnection between beauty, sexuality and gender, and by integrating these three in her life, comes to a place of understanding and comfort with who she is.

Compulsory Thinness: Are Lesbians Immune from the Barbie Mandate?

This section explores the way lesbians are affected by dominant cultural thinness standards. The authors examine lesbian attitudes and behaviors toward weight, appearance norms and dieting. In the first article, through a review of the literature and her own research, Karen Heffernan argues that lesbians are not immune from societal standards valuing thinness and that we suffer the consequences of these standards.

Gayle Pitman, in the second article, advances the theory that compulsory heterosexuality, internalized homophobia and fat oppression work together to promote poor body image. She criticizes the one-dimensional theories of eating disorders that fail to consider the experiences of women of color, working class women and lesbians.

Constance Guille and Joan Chrisler finish this section by presenting their own research concluding that cultural feminist messages, which include social and political solidarity for women and a celebration of womanhood, may protect against eating disorders.

OUR EXPECTATIONS AND REALITIES AS EDITORS

We began this publication with many expectations about what lesbians would say about beauty. Because we felt such freedom discarding dominant cultural beauty standards when we came out, we assumed others felt the same way. While we did receive many submissions on the strikingly different ways lesbians define beauty, a number of women also talked about how these definitions marginalized them.

We knew that lesbians were not exempt from body hatred, and expected some submissions on this topic, yet the number of submissions we received on body image issues surprised us. This debunks the notion that lesbians don't suffer from body hatred and eating disorders. The consistent voices of femme lesbians and the light they shed on the invisibility and lack of acceptance many of them experience equally surprised us.

Submissions we would have liked to receive include articles from lesbians who are differently abled, lesbians who identify themselves as butch, as well as lesbians bringing a working-class perspective to the publication. We also would have liked to learn more about the ways we express ourselves through dress and fashion. Due to Jeanine's training and network as a social scientist, the publication includes an over-representation of psychologists.

Our "wish list" illustrates that this publication can in no way be construed as a definitive exploration of lesbian beauty. We applaud the authors in this publication for their thorough analysis and eloquent insights. This work is a good start and we hope it is an impetus for further exploration.

WHAT WE LEARNED WORKING ON THIS PUBLICATION

The authors in this publication showed us the degree to which lesbians, ourselves included, use beauty norms to identify other lesbians, and to achieve a sense of belonging in our community. We were struck by Bonnie Strickland's discovery of a women's softball team as an adolescent and how their baseball caps and strong, competitive natures made her feel like she belonged for the first time in her life. We realized how much seeing other women with an appearance similar to ours makes us feel connected to our community.

Working on this publication forced us to challenge our own stereotypes about lesbian beauty. Perhaps we too are victims of a type of internalized sexism. Because we were made to feel weak when we dressed feminine, we perceived women who look or act femme as "weak" and women who appear androgynous or masculine as strong. This leads us to question how we can redefine feminine and masculine looks in lesbian culture without pandering to the definitions ascribed by the dominant culture. The feminine and masculine are not neutral; they each are cultural constructs laden with positive and negative meaning.

By creating this publication we have begun to acknowledge and push through our own clichés about lesbians and beauty; we are also raising compelling new questions. We vow to challenge our notions about appearance, and have a little more fun expressing our beauty as lesbians. We invite you to do the same. For us, that work has started. On an editing break, we set out on our first-ever clothes shopping expedition together and returned with blouses that one could safely call "pretty."

REFERENCES

Cogan, J.C. (1999). The social construction of eating disorders and obesity as pathological: Time to shift the model. In J. Sobal & D. Maurer (Eds.) *Interpreting Weight: The Social Management of Fatness and Thinness.* NY: Aldine de Gruyter Inc.

Deaux, K., & Hanna, R. (1984). Courtship in the personals column: The influence of gender and sexual orientation. *Sex Roles, 11*, 363-375.

Dew, M.A. (1985). The effect of attitudes on inferences of homosexuality and perceived physical attractiveness in women. *Sex Roles, 12*, 143-155.

Rothblum, E.D. (1994). Lesbians and psychological appearance: Which model applies? In B. Greene and G.M. Herek (Eds.) *Psychological Perspectives on Lesbian and Gay Issues, 1*, 84-97.

Unger, R.K., Hilderbrand, M., & Madar, T. (1982). Physical attractiveness and assumptions about social deviance: Some sex-by-sex comparisons. *Personality and Social Psychology Bulletin, 8*, 293-301.

PART I

IN THE EYE
OF THE BEHOLDER:
IDENTIFYING
AND DEFINING LESBIAN
BEAUTY NORMS

When thinking of lesbian beauty what comes up for me is the 'Michigan Women's Music Festival' from years ago in the sunlight, naked, beating drums, smiling and dancing. It is the unfolding of the journey in each of us; the journey from oppression. Also, how do I fit? I'm older now, settled 16 years with a partner and overweight–and I feel more beautiful than ever.

–Anonymous workshop
participant who was asked
"What do you think of when
you hear 'lesbian beauty'?"

Yeah, You

Carol Wuebker

She has the strength of workers at iron forges in her arms,
she is the water for a thousand parched lawns in Abu Dhabi,
she is the snow banked river in Montana,
she has magellanic clouds in her eyes.
She has the dexterity of a hundred-word-a minute typist in the manual
typewriter typist's pool.
Her feet have trodden paths
she never knew she would follow, Oregon trails not meant for debutantes.

She has flown above the Kamchatka peninsula and the forty-ninth
parallel, and never been shot down.
She's crossed the Rubicon in me, she can not go back.

(She'll never be
some stick figure
in
Elle or
Cosmo or
Vanity Fair.
They are fakes
and
pages are thin.)

Carol Wuebker is a computer geek living in Sacramento, California. She has a Bachelor of Science in German, which provides no end of amusement to her partner, Marjorie Gelus. They live happily in a little house in the suburbs with three cats.

Address correspondence to: Carol Wuebker, 2232 Ione Street, Sacramento, CA 95864.

[Haworth co-indexing entry note]: "Yeah, You." Wuebker, Carol. Co-published simultaneously in *Journal of Lesbian Studies* (The Haworth Press, Inc.) Vol. 3, No. 4, 1999, pp. 13-14; and: *Lesbians, Levis and Lipstick: The Meaning of Beauty in Our Lives* (ed: Jeanine C. Cogan and Joanie M. Erickson) The Haworth Press, Inc., 1999, pp. 13-14; and: *Lesbians, Levis and Lipstick: The Meaning of Beauty in Our Lives* (ed: Jeanine C. Cogan and Joanie M. Erickson) Harrington Park Press, an imprint of The Haworth Press, Inc., 1999, pp. 13-14. Single or multiple copies of this article are available for a fee from The Haworth Document Delivery Service [1-800-342-9678, 9:00 a.m. - 5:00 p.m. (EST). E-mail address: getinfo@haworthpressinc.com].

But she is my warm,
I know her by her scent and the touch of her skin,
her face is the first thing I seek when I walk in the door,
she is no icon.
She is flesh and beating heart and welcoming arms and sharp, like mind
and hello, how was your day,
and she has a body, and she has a soul, and she has a mind,
and she has my trust, and my comfort,
and my ebb and my flood,
she is my world geography, my world history, my major subject,
the first wonder of the world,
she is my most exotic journey,
and she is my coming back home.

Beauty Mandates
and the Appearance Obsession:
Are Lesbian and Bisexual Women
Better Off?

Anna Myers
Jennifer Taub
Jessica F. Morris
Esther D. Rothblum

Anna Myers is a writer and a doctoral student in the clinical psychology program at the University of Vermont. She writes short fiction, non-fiction, and poetry. Her professional research has focused on issues related to the psychology of women and to community mental health.

Jennifer Taub is a doctoral candidate in the clinical psychology program at the University of Vermont.

Jessica F. Morris recently received her PhD in clinical psychology from the University of Vermont and is a graduate of Vassar College. Her research, writing, and clinical work focus on the psychology of women, with an emphasis on lesbian studies. Her dissertation examined lesbian mental health and the coming out process.

Esther D. Rothblum is Professor of Psychology at the University of Vermont and editor of the *Journal of Lesbian Studies*. Her research focuses on lesbian studies and the stigma of women's weight.

Address correspondence to: Anna Myers, Department of Psychology, John Dewey Hall, University of Vermont, Burlington, VT 05405.

This article originally appeared in *Looking Queer: Body Image and Identity in Lesbian, Bisexual, Gay, and Transgender Communities* (Dawn Atkins, ed.). ©1998 by The Haworth Press, Inc.

[Haworth co-indexing entry note]: "Beauty Mandates and the Appearance Obsession: Are Lesbian and Bisexual Women Better Off?" Myers, Anna et al. Co-published simultaneously in *Journal of Lesbian Studies* (The Haworth Press, Inc.) Vol. 3, No. 4, 1999, pp. 15-26; and: *Lesbians, Levis and Lipstick: The Meaning of Beauty in Our Lives* (ed: Jeanine C. Cogan and Joanie M. Erickson) The Haworth Press, Inc., 1999, pp. 15-26; and: *Lesbians, Levis and Lipstick: The Meaning of Beauty in Our Lives* (ed: Jeanine C. Cogan and Joanie M. Erickson) Harrington Park Press, an imprint of The Haworth Press, Inc., 1999, pp. 15-26. Single or multiple copies of this article are available for a fee from The Haworth Document Delivery Service [1-800-342-9678, 9:00 a.m. - 5:00 p.m. (EST). E-mail address: getinfo@haworthpressinc.com].

SUMMARY. This article examines the effects of appearance norms within lesbian communities, drawing both on the research literature and on direct interviews with lesbian and bisexual women. In particular, the authors assess the impact of heterosexual beauty mandates on women's communities and ask whether lesbian and bisexual women are affected by the dominant culture's beauty mandates to a similar or lesser degree than heterosexual women. In addition, the authors examine appearance mandates developed by women within lesbian subculture. The positive and negative effects of these various "styles" on members of different lesbian subcultures are discussed. *[Article copies available for a fee from The Haworth Document Delivery Service: 1-800-342-9678. E-mail address: getinfo@ haworthpressinc.com]*

"Being female means being told how to look" (Rothblum, 1994, p. 84). For heterosexual women, the beauty standard is unavoidable: the images stare from magazines, billboards, TV screens, department store make-up counters–the list goes on. But what, if anything, does the heterosexual women's beauty ideal mean for women who are not heterosexual? To date, there has been little examination of the impact of the dominant culture's beauty standards on lesbian or bisexual communities. Prior to coming out, lesbian and bisexual women likely are pressured to conform to the same appearance norms as heterosexual women. Does coming out subsequently free lesbians and bisexuals from these norms, allowing them to find their own, unique styles? Or, is female beauty socialization carried over into lesbian and bisexual communities? Do these communities impose appearance standards of their own–standards perhaps as restrictive and narrow as heterosexual norms? Drawing on prior research, as well as on interviews with 20 lesbian and bisexual women from across the United States, this article examines ways in which female beauty mandates impact lesbian and bisexual women and raises questions about the relative freedom from such mandates currently experienced by these women in their own communities.

RESEARCH COMPARING LESBIAN AND HETEROSEXUAL WOMEN'S DISSATISFACTION WITH PHYSICAL APPEARANCE

Throughout their lives, all women are socialized to value a certain narrowly defined standard of physical attractiveness. Does this socialization persist after women discover that they are not heterosexual and begin to affiliate with lesbian and bisexual subcultures? We were unable to discover any empirical research to date which has directly addressed this question. Several studies, however, have compared heterosexual and lesbian women with regard to their level of satisfaction with their physical appearance.

Presumably, women are more satisfied with their bodies when their bodies conform to standards of what is generally considered "physically attractive." It has been hypothesized that the lesbian community protects women from body dissatisfaction because lesbian culture deemphasizes the importance of physical attractiveness (Beren, Hayden, Wilfley, & Grilo, 1996). If lesbians are freed from the tyranny of the heterosexual beauty standard, one would expect them to report more satisfaction with their diverse body types than heterosexual women. Results from studies comparing lesbian and heterosexual women's level of body dissatisfaction have not supported this hypothesis, however.

For example, Striegel-Moore, Tucker, and Hsu (1990) compared 30 lesbian and 52 heterosexual female undergraduates on measures of body esteem, self-esteem and disordered eating. Their research found no significant differences in body dissatisfaction between the two groups.

A second study by Herzog, Newman, Yeh, and Warshaw (1992) compared 45 lesbian and 64 heterosexual women with regard to body image, weight, eating attitudes and eating behaviors. They found that their sample of lesbians was significantly heavier and more satisfied with their overall appearance than their heterosexual sample. However, they also found that the two groups shared concerns about physical attractiveness and weight, in that both groups reported that they wanted to weigh less and considered thinner women to be more attractive than heavier women.

In a third study, Brand, Rothblum and Solomon (1992) compared levels of body dissatisfaction among 124 lesbians, 133 heterosexual women, 13 gay men, and 39 heterosexual men. The authors found that lesbian and heterosexual women reported significantly more dissatisfaction with their bodies than gay and heterosexual men–a finding which suggests that body dissatisfaction is just as prevalent among lesbians as among heterosexual women. The authors conclude that gender is a stronger predictor of body dissatisfaction than sexual orientation, in that women were more likely than men to be dissatisfied with their bodies–regardless of their sexual orientation.

A final study by Beren and colleagues (1996) compared 58 gay men, 58 heterosexual men, 69 lesbians and 72 heterosexual women on measures of body dissatisfaction. The authors found that again, lesbians and heterosexual women did not differ significantly with regard to body dissatisfaction, but that gay men were more dissatisfied with their appearance than heterosexual men.

While there is some disagreement among the findings of these four studies, overall it appears that lesbians report substantial levels of body dissatisfaction, and that their level of dissatisfaction is similar to the level reported by heterosexual women. While none of these studies included bisexual women, since gender is such an important variable in body image, it is likely that bisexual women are similarly dissatisfied with their bodies. If women's body dissatisfaction is seen as being the result of female socialization to accept a narrowly defined beauty ideal, it follows that these beauty ideals continue to affect women as they make the transition from heterosexual to lesbian and bisexual communities.

HISTORY OF APPEARANCE NORMS IN LESBIAN COMMUNITIES

An examination of lesbian history shows that lesbian communities have always had norms for physical appearance. Rothblum (1994) notes that, as the dominant culture's norms for female appearance have changed over time, so have the norms of the lesbian community. An important difference between the two norms, she says, is that while the dominant culture's norms have to do primarily with how women can attract men, lesbian norms have served a dual purpose: to allow lesbians to identify each other, and to provide a group identity that is distinct from that of women in the dominant culture.

In a review of U.S. lesbian history and culture in the 20th century, Faderman (1991) found appearance to be an important part of lesbian life. She notes that in the 1920s, being lesbian became chic among bohemian women. Black and white lesbians in Harlem and Greenwich Village began to form distinct subcultures, for which appearance lent a sense of group identity. Later, during World War II, women began to take factory jobs where they had to wear pants. This provided the opportunity for lesbians who hated dresses to continue to wear pants after the war, with less need to fear negative reactions.

By the 1950s, the butch/femme style emerged in lesbian communities. Although butch/femme culture encompassed far more than just a dress code, appearance was nevertheless a significant feature. Butch lesbians typically had short haircuts and wore man-tailored clothing, whereas femme lesbians tended to dress and groom themselves in a manner considered "feminine" for the time period. Butch/femme styles allowed lesbians to identify one another, as well as affording lesbians a way of expressing themselves as separate from the dominant culture. Among poor and working-class lesbians, butch/femme identity became a rigidly enforced code. Lesbians who were not clearly butch or femme were termed *kiki* and were unwelcome in places lesbians gathered. At least part of this rigidity had to do with fear. If a woman in a bar was not clearly butch or femme, other lesbians would be afraid to approach her lest she turned out to be a policewoman who did not "know how to dress."

In refusing to be invisible to the dominant culture, working-class and poor butch/femme lesbians paid the price for their "free" expression during all-too-common police raids and beatings. In contrast, middle-class and wealthy lesbians of the 1950s usually avoided butch/femme styles and were more likely to pass as heterosexual. Faderman (1991) quotes the Daughters of Bilitis' newsletter, which urged its middle-class readership to adopt "a mode of behavior and dress acceptable to society" (p. 180).

While the appearance norms of the dominant culture changed radically during the 1960s, Faderman reports that lesbian norms remained fairly constant until the dawning of the feminist movement in the 1970s. At this time, androgyny replaced butch/femme as the accepted appearance style. By dressing in an androgynous manner, women sought to distance themselves from the notion that [heterosexual] women should be a "decoration" for men. Women in lesbian communities were encouraged to dress for comfort and utility rather than to enhance their physical appearance in a style pleasing to heterosexual men. In rejecting the butch/femme aesthetic, lesbians of this time period also rejected the duality inherent in butch/femme roles: the mandate that one partner should be "masculine" and the other "feminine." This mandate began to be seen as patriarchal and oppressive. Lesbians of this time period sought to create more freedom for women to be themselves rather than to fit into a particular mold.

Loulan (1990) argues that, rather than creating more flexible appearance norms, lesbians of this time period simply created another oppressive norm. During the 1970s feminist movement, flannel shirts, blue jeans, work boots, an absence of jewelry or makeup, and short hair became *de rigueur*. Among lesbians, this norm was as rigidly enforced as the butch/femme code had been enforced in the years prior. Loulan describes how butch/femme lesbians of this time period were ostracized for aping heterosexual styles, and how this attitude persists in lesbian communities today.

According to Rothblum (1994), the 1980s and 1990s have reflected greater diversity in the lesbian community. She points out that in the last 20 years, lesbians of a variety of ethnicities and cultures have become more visible to the dominant culture, often forming communities of their own. Additionally, butch/femme styles have undergone a renaissance. The sadomasochist (S/M) subculture, which has its own style of dress and behavior, has become more visible. In the last 20 years, then, it is possible that lesbian and bisexual women have begun to be less rigid in the extent to which they hold one another to standards of "appropriate" appearance and behavior.

The authors cited above describe several ways that appearance standards do exist within lesbian communities.[1] Historical analyses suggest that lesbians have always paid attention to physical appearance in order to feel attractive and also to identify one another and/or to make a political statement. However, the question still remains whether female socialization to value certain standards of appearance persists after women come out.

DO APPEARANCE NORMS PERSIST AFTER WOMEN COME OUT?

In attempting to examine the question about the durability of the heterosexual beauty standard in women's communities, we interviewed 18 lesbian and 2 bisexual women about their experience of appearance norms in lesbian communities. Specifically, we asked whether they believed that their communities held women to certain appearance standards, and if so, whether those appearance standards were any more or less restrictive than heterosexual appearance norms. Our interviews took place in person, by telephone, and over electronic mail. Our respondents were 20 women whose ages ranged from 17 to 60 years old (Mean = 32). Of those women who shared their racial or ethnic heritage, 12 identified as white, 1 as Latina, and 1 as mixed-race.

Because our sample size is small, no definitive conclusions about appearance norms in lesbian communities can be drawn from these interviews; however, they may uncover themes worthy of further investigation. Additionally, it is not possible to generalize from the experience of these women to all lesbian and bisexual women. However, our respondents were able to tell us what they experienced to be the norms regarding physical appearance within their local lesbian communities.

To some extent, our interviews supported the research findings that lesbians and bisexual women continue to be affected by female appearance norms even after coming out. Said one lesbian:

> Let's face it. The traditional standards of beauty for women are basically the same whether you're gay, straight, bisexual, or whatever. Looksism is as strong in the lesbian community as anywhere, if not more so. Women are more critical of other women than men are.

Said another woman:

> I get a lot of crap, hostility, anger, and bullshit like that from other lesbians because I'm an extremely butch woman–very masculine looking. . . . Lesbians are very good at turning on each other. I haven't had positive experiences in the lesbian community.

These two women seem to express a feeling that lesbians and bisexuals can be just as judgmental as heterosexuals in creating appearance standards.

However, other respondents reported feeling freed from beauty norms after coming out. A number of women interviewed remarked that there is greater acceptance of physical appearances not consistent with the dominant culture's norms within the lesbian community. They reported feeling freer both to abandon traditional female appearance styles and to experiment more with those styles.

For example, one woman remarked:

> After I came out, I started to question the clothing I wore, the style of my hair, jewelry, make-up, the playing dumb thing. I cut off all my hair, I stopped shaving my legs and armpits, I stopped wearing make-up, and

> I literally burned my bra. I exchanged my sandals and pumps for an attractive pair of construction boots. I felt stronger, even more powerful than I had before. I wasn't playing dumb; I was playing tough.

Said another:

> [After] I moved into a lesbian household, [a housemate] introduced me to lace and lingerie. I found out that as a lesbian–a femme lesbian–I could celebrate my body. I could *be* in my body for the first time. I could look in the mirror and have what I saw be okay. Be more than okay–be fantastic! For me, femme is the strongest, most powerful place I can be.

Another woman echoed this feeling of freedom:

> When I look at [heterosexual] women my age, they look frumpy. I'm glad I don't have to look like them.

Thus, while the idea that lesbians and bisexual women are less affected by the dominant culture's beauty mandate was not universally accepted among the women interviewed for this article, the theme of "freedom" from heterosexual appearance norms after coming out was a unifying factor. This seeming contradiction–that lesbian and bisexual women are freed from the dominant culture's beauty norms yet still are judgmental of one another's physical appearance–raised other questions. How do beauty mandates creep into lesbian communities? Are lesbian and bisexual women truly freed from appearance norms, or do they merely set up their own norms in opposition to those of the dominant culture? While appearance norms in lesbian communities differ from heterosexual norms, are these different norms any less rigid?

We concluded that the question of whether lesbian communities hold their members to appearance norms as restrictive as those in the dominant culture cannot be answered in a straightforward manner. Our interviews suggest that women's experience of the restrictiveness of appearance norms in their communities depended in large measure on other variables. These variables included body weight of the woman being interviewed, her age and length of time since coming out, and her membership in certain subcultures within the lesbian community (such as butch/femme or S/M subcultures).

With regard to body weight, several of our respondents reported that they found lesbian communities to be more accepting of larger-sized women. Said one fat respondent:

> My feminist and lesbian political awareness tell me that I am accepted for all that I am–mind, body and soul. . . . I don't feel restricted at this point to one standard of beauty.

However, this woman continued to say that even within a more accepting lesbian-feminist community, she still struggled with trying to accept her own body size due to her socialization within the dominant culture.

A bisexual woman we interviewed said that she experienced the "fat acceptance" rhetoric within her own women's community to be somewhat restrictive in and of itself. As someone who was trying to lose weight, she felt that her personal choice was not accepted by other lesbian and bisexual women. She told us:

> I am not at all happy with my weight right now. [In my community], I sort of feel like I am supposed to "come out as fat," when *I* do not feel comfortable being that way and am trying to change it. I think that fat acceptance is a stronger issue in the queer community than elsewhere, and I don't have a problem with that. What makes me feel funny is the [implication that being fat] is something you are supposed to be happy about and proud of, when I'm neither happy nor proud.

Thus, women like this one still experience the "fat acceptance" standard as confining and limiting.

These two women's experiences echo the research findings cited earlier, which suggest that despite an apparent relaxation of beauty standards, lesbian and bisexual women still report substantial levels of body dissatisfaction. For the two women quoted above, body dissatisfaction was more related to heterosexual appearance standards which value thinness than to beauty standards within women's communities.

Age and length of time since coming out also greatly affected the degree to which the lesbians and bisexual women we interviewed felt they needed to conform to appearance norms. Younger and newly-out women felt more appearance pressure than did older women and women who had been out for a number of years. Two lesbians over 40, for example, expressed great satisfaction with their overall appearance:

> I've been out for 15 years. As a sick, fat, middle-aged woman, being a lesbian is a wonderful gift. I love my aging body!

Said the second woman:

> I'm an outspoken dyke activist. I have no "clothes dilemmas." At work I wear comfortable cotton pants, blazer, white shirts. . . . I can always tell the straight women: they're the ones wearing sweaters.

Women who had been "out" for a number of years echoed the feelings of the older women. They told us that they felt freer to dress however they liked once they had solidified their lesbian or bisexual identity and established themselves within their local communities. For example, a bisexual woman who told us that she has been "out" for a decade said:

> As I've gotten older . . . it has become less necessary for me to blend in with the queer community. I know I'm queer now, and I don't need everyone else to be able to see it when they look at me.

Likewise, a lesbian who said she "played tough" right after coming out, stated:

> I no longer own a flannel shirt. My construction boots are buried under pumps and granny boots. I wear lipstick and my hair is long.

In contrast to the experience of older women and women who had been out for a number of years, comments by teen-aged, newly-out lesbians reflected frustration with lesbian appearance norms and anxiety about "fitting in." Said one teenager:

> In the lesbian community, people stereotype you based on what you wear. If you wear leather, you're classified as a "butch leather queen." If you dress like me, you're femme. . . . They want to make sure that people in their group meet all their requirements. It's very excluding.

Said another:

> I dress differently [since coming out] . . . more pants, less skirts, no dresses . . . no heels. My hair is much shorter. I have also noticed that if I'm going to a festival or a women-only event I choose what I wear carefully. I think about it, which I normally wouldn't do.

It may be that women feel more pressure to "fit in" and to be "recognizably lesbian" when they first come out, especially if they are actively dating. Later, and perhaps after finding a partner, women feel freer to express their personal styles.

Another theme that emerged in our interviews was a feeling that a variety of appearance norms exist within various subcultures of the lesbian community, with corresponding pressures to conform to each norm. For example, contrast the responses of several women to the question, "Is there a lesbian aesthetic?" Two women summarized the "androgynous" aesthetic well. Said one:

> I think there's a general aesthetic. It hasn't changed much since the 70s. It's the androgynous look: short hair, round glasses, scarf around the

neck. Some wear earrings, some wear leather jackets, some wear denim
. . . There are different versions, but they are all based on the same
template.

Said another:

I think there's more tolerance for some types of "appearance" (e.g.,
facial hair, overweight, man-tailored clothing), but there is also so much
suspiciousness about traditionally "feminine" norms of dress.

The "androgynous" aesthetic, however, was not seen as being an appearance mandate within lesbian communities. Subcultures within the community, in particular the butch/femme subculture, were said to set their own appearance norms. One woman, who identified as a butch lesbian, told us:

There's a butch standard. The classic butch is a diesel dyke: crew cut,
broad shoulders, no tits, slim hips, able to pass as a man . . . If you say
"femme," people will say she has long hair, wears skirts, makeup,
heels . . .

Women who identified as butch and femme complained that, while they
might be accepted within their own butch/femme circles, they had trouble
fitting in to the larger lesbian community. Some of these women hypothesized that, because they represent a challenge to the "androgynous" lesbian
aesthetic, they face harassment and exclusion. For example, a woman who
identified as femme told us:

Femmes are not accepted because they're treated as if they are trying to
pass as straight. [They] lose the support, the contact that may occur.

Thus, what the butch/femme lesbians seem to be saying is that appearance
norms do exist within lesbian communities. Women who identify as butch or
femme dress in certain ways that are accepted within their own subculture of the
community, but they do not necessarily feel accepted within the larger women's
community, which may value a different, more "androgynous" aesthetic.

CONCLUSION

Lesbian appearance norms are clearly different from heterosexual ones;
however, the beauty mandate of the dominant culture has apparently been
reproduced to some extent within women's communities. The heterosexual
beauty mandate continues to affect lesbians and bisexual women to the extent

that they continue to worry about weight and other factors that make up the dominant culture's ideal.

In addition, lesbians and bisexuals seem to create norms within lesbian communities. The degree to which women feel pressured to conform to such norms may be a factor of age and years "out," just as the degree to which heterosexual women conform to the dominant culture's norms changes over time. Other factors influencing the pressure to conform or not may be membership in a subculture, such as the butch/femme subculture. Women in such subcultures may experience less acceptance by the larger lesbian community, and they might create different norms for appearance in their own groups.

Thus, while in theory lesbian communities give women the chance to define themselves and find the appearance they find most pleasing to themselves, our research suggests that appearance norms continue to exist among lesbians and bisexuals. Some women experience these norms as being just as restrictive as those of the dominant culture. As one lesbian we interviewed noted, it is ironic that a group which has so emphasized eschewing the heterosexual beauty aesthetic creates beauty standards of its own. Said she: "On a personal level, I find it all pretty tiresome." It seems that for lesbian and bisexual women, as for heterosexuals, appearance norms are a fact of life, and mere identification as lesbian or bisexual is not enough to free women from appearance mandates.

NOTE

1. Once again, this theoretical work has not specifically addressed appearance norms among bisexual women. In fact, the existence of bisexual women's community itself is a relatively recent phenomenon, and therefore research on issues unique to bisexuals is scant. (We refer you to Taub, this volume.)

REFERENCES

Beren, S.E., Hayden, H.A., Wilfley, D.E., & Grilo, C.M. (1996). The influence of sexual orientation on body dissatisfaction in adult men and women. *International Journal of Eating Disorders, 20*, 135-141.

Brand, P.A., Rothblum, E.D., & Solomon, L.A. (1992). A comparison of lesbians, gay men, and heterosexuals on weight and restrained eating. *International Journal of Eating Disorders, 11*, 253-259.

Faderman, L. (1991). *Odd Girls and Twilight Lovers: A History of Lesbian Life in Twentieth-Century America*. New York: Columbia University Press.

Herzog, D.B., Newman, K.L., Yeh, C.J. & Warshaw, M. (1992). Body image satisfaction in homosexual and heterosexual women. *International Journal of Eating Disorders, 11*, 391-396.

Loulan, J.A. (1990). *The Lesbian Erotic Dance: Butch, Femme, Androgyny, and Other Rhythms*. San Francisco: Spinster.

Rothblum, E.D. (1994). Lesbians and physical appearance: Which model applies? In B. Greene and G.M. Herek (Eds.), *Psychological Perspectives on Lesbian and Gay Issues, 1*, 84-97.

Striegel-Moore, R.H., Tucker, N., & Hsu, J. (1990). Body image dissatisfaction and disordered eating in lesbian college students. *International Journal of Eating Disorders, 9*, 493-500.

Bisexual Women and Beauty Norms:
A Qualitative Examination

Jennifer Taub

SUMMARY. This article examines how coming out and gender of partner affect bisexual women's behavior, thoughts and feelings regarding beauty and appearance norms. Seventy-four bisexual women participated in a qualitative survey addressing these issues. Results showed that just under half (49%) of respondents felt that coming out as bisexual affected their beauty ideas and practices and over two-thirds (71%) felt that the gender of their partners affected their beauty ideas and practices. Most of the latter group (80%) felt more appearance pressures when involved with men than when involved with women. Themes from open-ended responses are presented through specific examples and the implications of findings are discussed. *[Article copies available for a fee from The Haworth Document Delivery Service: 1-800-342-9678. E-mail address: getinfo@haworthpressinc.com]*

Virtually no attention has been paid to the ways in which appearance expectations of the dominant culture impact bisexual women. Research examining sexual orientation and body image (comparing heterosexuals to

Jennifer Taub is a doctoral student in the Clinical Psychology program at the University of Vermont. Her various research interests include bisexuality, children's mental health services, empowerment, and prevention programs.

Address correspondence to: Jennifer Taub, Department of Psychology, John Dewey Hall, Burlington, VT 05405 (E-mail: jtaub@zoo.uvm.edu).

The author wishes to thank Lynne Bond and Anna Myers for their editing assistance, helpful feedback and suggestions.

[Haworth co-indexing entry note]: "Bisexual Women and Beauty Norms: A Qualitative Examination." Taub, Jennifer. Co-published simultaneously in *Journal of Lesbian Studies* (The Haworth Press, Inc.) Vol. 3, No. 4, 1999, pp. 27-36; and: *Lesbians, Levis and Lipstick: The Meaning of Beauty in Our Lives* (ed: Jeanine C. Cogan and Joanie M. Erickson) The Haworth Press, Inc., 1999, pp. 27-36; and: *Lesbians, Levis and Lipstick: The Meaning of Beauty in Our Lives* (ed: Jeanine C. Cogan and Joanie M. Erickson) Harrington Park Press, an imprint of The Haworth Press, Inc., 1999, pp. 27-36. Single or multiple copies of this article are available for a fee from The Haworth Document Delivery Service [1-800-342-9678, 9:00 a.m. - 5:00 p.m. (EST). E-mail address: getinfo@haworthpressinc.com].

lesbians and gay men, no data on bisexuals) (Beren, Hayden, Wilfley & Grilo, 1996; Brand, Rothblum & Solomon, 1992; Herzog, Newman, Yeh & Warshaw, 1992; Striegel-Moore, Tucker & Hsu, 1990) found that to some extent lesbians strive toward the stereotypically thin beauty standard for women (see Heffernan, this volume). Other research (see Cogan, this volume; Myers, Taub, Morris & Rothblum, this volume) suggests that while lesbians continue to be affected by the dominant culture's appearance norms after coming out, they also experience greater acceptance within lesbian communities of physical appearances not consistent with the dominant culture's norms. This suggests that lesbians have their own beauty standards within their communities, standards that differ from heterosexual ones. Rothblum (1994) hypothesized that women who are not in sexual relationships with men may find standard appearance norms less important because one of the primary reasons women seek to attain such ideals is to attract male partners.

If it is true that a distinct lesbian beauty standard exists, are bisexual women more likely to endorse heterosexual or lesbian beauty standards? Although research has not addressed this specific question, sociologist Paula Rust's (1995) study examining bisexual women's preferences for affiliation can shed some light on this issue. She found that the more heterosexually oriented bisexual women were, the more they preferred to socialize with other bisexuals, while the more homosexually oriented they were, the more they preferred to affiliate with lesbians. Further, bisexual women who were involved in relationships with lesbians were more likely to work for lesbian political concerns and endorse lesbian candidates than were bisexual women who were involved with men. Extrapolating from this research and incorporating the idea that physical appearance is a way to attract others with whom one wishes to socialize and date, it would follow that bisexual women who are currently involved with women or who identify more homosexually than heterosexually would adhere more to lesbian beauty standards; bisexual women who are involved with men or who identify more heterosexually would adhere more to heterosexual appearance norms. The purpose of this study was to examine how coming out as bisexual and gender of one's partner influenced bisexual women's appearance.

PRESENT STUDY

Sample

Seventy-seven bisexual women responded to a survey through bisexual or gay/lesbian/bisexual mailing lists on the Internet, friendship networks, bisexual organizations, and a snowball technique, where individuals passed along surveys to other bisexual women they thought might be interested in participating. The criteria for inclusion in this study were that participants were female, at least 18 years of age, and currently self-identified as bisexual.

In response to the question "What is your racial and/or ethnic identification?" sixty-eight women (88%) identified themselves as white, four (5%) as Asian-American, three (4%) as bi- or multiracial, one (1%) as African-American and one (1%) as Latina. Nine women (12%) described themselves as Jewish in addition to white. Participants ranged in age from 18 to 47 (median = 29). The average number of years they had been out as bisexual to themselves was 9.3 years (range 1-29 years), and to others was 7.6 years (range 1-25 years). The mean age at coming out to oneself was 20 and to others was 22.

Fifty-five women (71%) said they were currently partnered or dating, and of these, thirty-two (58%) had a male partner or partners, twenty (36%) had a female partner, and three (5%) had both a male and a female partner.

Procedure

Through a written questionnaire, participants were asked open-ended questions about the impact of coming out as bisexual, and of gender of partner on bisexual women's experience regarding appearance norms or beauty rituals. Participants were asked: (1) Did any of these items (being thin, dieting, bleaching/removing body hair, wearing make-up, working out, piercing/tattooing/body art, anything else related to body or beauty) change for you when you came out as bi? (2) Do you think that appearance norms or beauty standards have played different roles in your life when involved with a man or men vs. involved with a woman or women?

Methods of Qualitative Data Analysis

Methods for analysis of qualitative data as outlined and discussed by Strauss (1987) were used. For each of the two questions the author employed open coding. Open coding is an unrestricted coding procedure to determine categories that fit the data through line by line readings resulting in the generation of sets of theoretical categories. Open coding was done twice, and the categories that were generated both times were subject to further analyses. Axial coding, an intensive coding procedure around each category, was then used to identify themes. Both in-vivo (using the language of the participants) and sociological (formulated by the author) codes were identified, and given code names. Categories containing theoretically fundamental similarities were collapsed. Results are discussed below.

Appearance Norms and Coming Out

Does coming out as bisexual affect women's beauty or appearance ideas and practices? Participants were asked to discuss the importance of a number of appearance-related behaviors (i.e., dieting, removal of body hair, piercing/ tattooing) in their lives, and if any of these behaviors had changed for them when they came out as bisexual. Of the sixty-nine respondents who answered this question, half of these women (n = 34) said that there were changes when they came out as bisexual and half (n = 35) said there were not. For those who offered answers their responses fell into five categories: (1) giving up beauty rituals, (2) increased acceptance of own appearance, (3) adopting heterosexual norms, (4) adopting lesbian norms, and (5) feeling less pressure to conform to dominant appearance norms.

Giving Up Beauty Rituals

Almost a third of women (29%; n = 10) who reported some change in appearance after they came out as bisexual, gave up certain beauty rituals such as shaving body hair and wearing make-up. These women reported actually changing their beauty-related behavior after coming out. As one woman said, "It was part of a coming out process as queer to stop shaving." Another woman noted that "I think I stopped caring virtually at all about make-up."

Increased Acceptance of Own Appearance

Six (18%) women reported that coming out as bisexual led to increased self-acceptance about their appearance. According to one 25-year-old woman, "As I realized who I found attractive, I began to apply different beauty standards to myself." And a 31-year-old explained, "Enjoying the wonderful softness of other women enables me to see the positive potential of my extra pounds."

Adopting Heterosexual Norms

Interestingly, five women (15%) said that they adopted more traditionally feminine styles when they came out as bisexual. Four of these five women noted that they had come out as bisexual from a lesbian sexual orientation, rather than from heterosexual identities. These women spoke of adopting more "femme" styles, or being able to explore more feminine aspects of themselves that they felt less able to explore when identified as lesbian. For example, one 37-year-old woman explained,

> Coming out as bi probably gave me permission to deviate from the traditional "butch" lesbian look and allowed me to hold on to some of my femininity which is such a part of me–for better or worse. Before that time I didn't feel I belonged to either camp and looked toward

androgyny for some guidance. After coming out as bi I felt it was OK to affirm all aspects of myself–to wear dresses and jeans, earrings and boots . . . depending on how I felt at the time. It's as if coming out as bi gave me permission to be "me" on many levels.

A 39-year-old bisexual woman who had identified as lesbian for a decade said, "Initially when I came out [as lesbian] I stopped shaving and doing make up. Then I resumed it in my late 20's as I explored femme identity." She noted that she enjoyed challenging the "lesbian stereotype" she felt she had adopted. Another woman, previously identified as lesbian, noted that she started shaving after coming out as bisexual to please her male partner, which she had not done when lesbian identified.

Adopting Lesbian Norms

Four women (12%) adopted more androgynous or butch appearances after coming out as bisexual. Of these women, one said that she became more androgynous in appearance, and three said they became more "butch" or "dykey" in appearance. For example, one 40-year-old woman said,

I have a dyke look that I assume when I want to fit in more with lesbian social settings, and I think I've been more careful about keeping my haircut very crisp and clean so I can look more dykey when I want to instead of letting it go longer and shaggier.

Less Pressure to Conform to Dominant Cultural Norms

Four (12%) of the respondents who reported changes after coming out as bisexual noted that they had come to feel less overall pressure to conform to the appearance norms expected of women. These women did not report altering their beauty-related behavior, but they reported feeling differently about the beauty norms of the dominant culture. A 40-year-old explained that, "Body image seemed not quite such an issue" after coming out. And a 30-year-old said, "When I identified as straight, I felt more pressure (external) to be thin, shave and wear make up. When I came out there was less external pressure to diet, wear make up, etc."

Other Responses

The remaining five women (15%) who experienced changes in their appearance-related behavior after coming out as bisexual gave responses that could not be coded into any of the above categories. For example, one woman said that her bisexuality affected her haircuts and tattoo choices. Another woman, partnering with men, said that she began to pay more attention to her appearance after coming out as bisexual since she was "out in the dating scene again."

Women vs. Men, or How the Gender of One's Partner Affects Beauty Ideas

Does the gender of one's partner affect bisexual women's beauty or appearance ideas and practices? According to this sample, the overwhelming sentiment was that it does. Of the 65 women responding to this question, 71% (n = 46) said that appearance norms or beauty standards played different roles in their lives when involved with men versus women; the remaining 29% (n = 19) indicated that gender made no difference.

Gender Makes a Difference

The responses of the 46 respondents who noted differences in their behaviors or attitudes about beauty and appearance based on gender of partner, fell into four different categories: (1) feeling more pressure to conform to heterosexual beauty standards with men, (2) feeling free from appearance pressures with women, (3) adopting lesbian beauty norms with women, and (4) feeling appearance pressures with women. Respondents' answers could be coded in one or more of the categories.

More pressure to conform to heterosexual beauty standards with men. Of the women reporting that gender of partner does make a difference, 83% (n = 38) spoke of feeling more pressure to conform to "feminine" beauty standards with men than with women, either currently or in the past.

Of these women, fifteen (40%) noted that they felt unique pressure to attend to appearance when with male partners, either from their partners, or from themselves. One woman said, "When I am involved with a man I feel like I have to present myself better, like I have to prove that I am a pretty enough woman for him." Another woman wrote, "I find that when I'm involved with men, I tend to fall more into the heterosexual beauty-norm game . . . I become interested and willing to wear what men are supposed to find sexy, etc." And a 34-year-old commented, "When involved with a man I feel more internal pressure to look attractive in the way that the straight culture dictates women should look. I do not feel this pressure when involved with a woman." Without mentioning specific beauty practices, a woman said, "When I'm with a guy, I feel a lot more feminine and in general, I think about my appearance more. [When dating a woman] it was a lot more relaxed, whereas guys wanted to see a perfect finished product."

Fifteen women (40%) noted specifically altering their appearance when dating men to conform to more feminine norms. For example, one woman wrote, "Many [heterosexual] men prefer a more feminine girl, which hasn't really come up with women. Men are more likely to want leg and underarm hair shaved, which I'll do." Another woman said, simply, "I wear more feminine clothes with a man." Seven women also felt that, in the words of a 31-year-old, "In general, weight has been more of an issue with men than with women."

Less appearance pressures with women. Rather than addressing the pressures about appearance with men, sixteen women (42%) specifically noted the positive or empowering experience of the lessened appearance pressures with women partners. Regarding weight, a 30-year-old wrote, "Women partners have been much more accepting (even enthusiastic) about my big body. Whereas my male partners have been tolerant at first and learned to love my body." A 28-year-old explained, "I feel like the least accepting woman is going to be more accepting of my [physical] shortcomings than the most accepting man." Such feelings of acceptance of their physical selves allowed some of these women to feel more comfortable with themselves overall in their relationships with women. According to one 30-year-old, "[Heterosexual] appearance norms and beauty standards held me back from appreciating myself. Being with an affirming female lover crushed their power and set me free." A 23-year-old said simply, "I feel more beautiful because I feel comfortable and I feel like women don't obsess about other women's bodies as much as men do."

Adopting lesbian beauty norms. Nine women (24%) said they adopted some degree of lesbian beauty norms for various reasons. Of these women, seven were currently partnered with a man, and two with a woman. One woman commented that she felt pressure to adopt lesbian beauty norms in order to be accepted when she is not involved with a woman. She said,

> When dating a specific woman I can look pretty much however I want (so long as I'm projecting a coherent and either clever or lesbian-mainstream style). The problem comes with lesbians when I'm *not* dating a woman. Then I feel I have to dress anti-heterosexually to prove I'm really a dyke (which I'm not, I'm bi, but there's a fair bit of bi-phobia in the lesbian community).

A 35-year-old who was partnered with a man described her appearance and its perception by other women:

> Now I'm just uninterested in what men think about me appearance-wise. Expectations and needs of women are more likely to influence me now, not to change my appearance but to feel emotions about it. Sometimes when women look at my loose androgynous clothing, short hair,

etc., they assume I'm lesbian and react to me accordingly, either to communicate acceptance, to approach me sexually, or to display disapproval or threatened feeling. . . . I think that gender markers and sexual signals are important to our culture.

Four of these nine women also endorsed adopting more of the dominant culture's beauty norms when involved with men. For example, a 24-year-old explained,

I find that when I'm involved with men, I tend to fall more into the heterosexual beauty-norm game. I become interested and willing to wear what men are supposed to find sexy. And when involved with women, I tend to fall more into working with the lesbian or bi beauty norms.

Two of these women expressed how they adopted more femme roles when dating women, but not when dating men. A 37-year-old said, "When dating women, especially butch women, I feel very comfortable being more feminine" and a 31-year-old commented, "[I was] more conscious of wearing dresses and playing into the femme role with women."

Appearance pressure with women. Five women (13%) noted feeling more pressures with women than men regarding appearance. The women who spoke of feeling these pressures with other women fell into one of two groups: either they cared more about women's opinions and were therefore more likely to alter their appearance to please women, or they felt judged by women for attempting to explore femme identities. One woman who exemplified the former says,

I must say that I feel more comfortable around men with my body than around women; especially women I've been involved with. Perhaps I care about their opinion more? . . . I've been more self-conscious around women, so I'm more careful about the way I appear than with men.

Another woman who says she used to "worry about being attractive to males," and therefore tailored her appearance to "normative heterosexual beauty norms" notes that currently she is more concerned about tailoring her appearance to women. A 39-year-old woman expressed her bitterness at feeling appearance pressure with women. She said,

Actually, I got less support for presenting myself as femme (an identity I very much wanted to explore) when I was with women. In general I have felt *women* to be somewhat more judgmental (author italics).

Gender of Partner Does Not Make a Difference

As already noted, nineteen (29%) of the women responding to this question said that they did not feel the gender of their partner had an impact on the role of appearance norms in their lives. A few women said that the person, rather than the gender, is important to them. For example, a 24-year-old wrote,

> I am in a non-monogamous relationship with a bi man. He is the first man who ever told me I was beautiful. So he was a major factor in increasing my self-esteem around my appearance. I have dated several fat women while in this relationship, and seeing them as beautiful, and knowing they thought I was beautiful has also been a huge factor.

Other women felt that their self-image and beauty practices remained stable and were unrelated to their partner's gender or individual characteristics. For example, a 31-year-old woman said, "I'm pretty much a femme top and my image has not changed much in either my relationships with men or women." Said another, "I've tended to look the same regardless of my partner's gender."

CONCLUSION

Results from this study suggest that for many women in this sample, both coming out as bisexual and the gender of one's partner influenced their behaviors and attitudes about beauty norms and appearance.

Since the majority of women in this sample felt pressure to adhere to dominant, heterosexual, beauty norms at some point in their lives, it comes as no surprise that a majority of these women felt more pressures to conform to heterosexual standards when involved in heterosexual relationships, than lesbian relationships. There was also a clear sentiment that women as partners were more accepting of women's appearance, leading many women to feel more comfortable about their bodies and appearance in their relationships with women than in their relationships with men. However, some women reported differentially changing their appearance-related behavior to attract or please men or women at various points. As one woman said, "The roles are different, but the role-playing is the same." It may simply be that many women alter appearance to attract the object of their desire, adopting whichever "norms" they presume the object to find attractive.

There are limitations to this study. Although geographically diverse, the sample in this study did not include older bisexual women (older than 50) and had a high proportion of white respondents. Further, respondents tended to be affiliated with, or friends and acquaintances of, women in groups and bisexual organizations who were more likely to be out. Future research in this area that includes more diverse samples of bisexual women would add greatly to the knowledge of how various factors such as ethnicity, age, and outness affect bisexual women's self-perceptions of beauty and appearance.

REFERENCES

Beren, S.E., Hayden, H.A., Wilfley, D.E. & Grilo, C.M. (1996). The influence of sexual orientation on body dissatisfaction in adult men and women. *International Journal of Eating Disorders, 20*, 135-141.

Brand, P.A., Rothblum, E.D. & Solomon, L.J. (1992). A comparison of lesbians, gay men, and heterosexuals on weight and restrained eating. *Int'l Journal of Eating Disorders, 11*(3) 253-259.

Herzog, D.B., Newman, K.L., Yeh, C.J. & Warshaw, M. (1992). Body image satisfaction in homosexual and heterosexual women. *Int'l Journal of Eating Disorders, 11*(4) 391-396.

Rothblum, E.D. (1994). Lesbians and physical appearance: Which model applies? In B. Greene and G.M. Herek (Eds.), *Psychological Perspectives on Lesbian and Gay Issues, 1*, 84-97.

Rust, P. (1995). *Bisexuality and the Challenge to Lesbian Politics*. New York: New York University Press.

Strauss, A.L. (1987). *Qualitative Analysis for Social Scientists*. Cambridge: Cambridge University Press.

Striegel-Moore, R.H., Tucker, N. & Hsu, J. (1990). Body image dissatisfaction and disordered eating in lesbian college students. *Int'l Journal of Eating Disorders, 9*, 493-500.

Lesbians Discuss Beauty and Aging

Kim M. Thompson
Nancy Brown
Joan Cassidy
Jacqueline H. Gentry

SUMMARY. Two conversations with three aging lesbians are presented to identify and explore different definitions of beauty and how these
definitions change and are influenced by age. The three women interviewed believe beauty is more than skin deep, yet they differ regarding
specific components of beauty. Two believe that their definition of
beauty has changed as they age and one believes that her definition has
remained basically unchanged through the years. Topics of discussion
include: beauty role models, the impact of the American beauty standard on their self-esteem, and what they look for in potential partners.
Through these women's diverse opinions on how beauty is defined and
experienced by older lesbians, we see that there is no one perspective
representing all older women. *[Article copies available for a fee from The
Haworth Document Delivery Service: 1-800-342-9678. E-mail address: getinfo@
haworthpressinc.com]*

Kim M. Thompson is a third-year graduate student in the Clinical Psychology
Department at the University of Maryland, College Park.

Nancy Brown took early retirement from the Division of AIDS, National Institute
of Allergy and Infectious Diseases and is now active in traveling with an RV (Recre-
ational Vehicle) group.

Joan Cassidy took early retirement from the Naval Security Station in Washington, DC, and is currently acting in community theatre productions.

Jacquelyn H. Gentry is Director of Public Interest Initiatives for the APA and is
currently writing a book about the wisdom and talents of old women.

Address correspondence to: Kim M. Thompson, Department of Psychology, University of Maryland, College Park, MD 20742-4411.

[Haworth co-indexing entry note]: "Lesbians Discuss Beauty and Aging." Thompson, Kim M. et al.
Co-published simultaneously in *Journal of Lesbian Studies* (The Haworth Press, Inc.) Vol. 3, No. 4, 1999,
pp. 37-44; and: *Lesbians, Levis and Lipstick: The Meaning of Beauty in Our Lives* (ed: Jeanine C. Cogan
and Joanie M. Erickson) The Haworth Press, Inc., 1999, pp. 37-44; and: *Lesbians, Levis and Lipstick: The
Meaning of Beauty in Our Lives* (ed: Jeanine C. Cogan and Joanie M. Erickson) Harrington Park Press, an
imprint of The Haworth Press, Inc., 1999, pp. 37-44. Single or multiple copies of this article are available for
a fee from The Haworth Document Delivery Service [1-800-342-9678, 9:00 a.m. - 5:00 p.m. (EST). E-mail
address: getinfo@haworthpressinc.com].

This article describes conversations with three aging lesbians who identify and explore their definitions of beauty and how these definitions change and are influenced by age.

THE CAST OF CHARACTERS

Interviewer: Kim Thompson is 26 years old. She was born and raised in Washington, DC, and was educated in the DC public school system. She attended undergraduate college at the University of Wisconsin, Madison campus. Here she was involved in many different projects, such as being a peaceful witness in Northern Wisconsin when the Chippewa tribe was attempting to exercise their treaty rights to spearfish. She photographed and tape recorded this event to document the opposition's assaults on the tribe. She also worked at two chapters of the Rape Crisis Center. She received her BA in both Psychology and Anthropology. After graduating from college, she played in punk music bands that toured the United States four times and released several records. Three years later, she entered the Clinical Psychology doctoral program at the University of Maryland, College Park, where she is currently a third-year student. Her research interests include forensic psychology and the mental health of women exiting welfare.

Respondents: Nancy Brown, age 57, was born in Jackson, Mississippi. In childhood, she quickly became adept with mechanical objects, including baiting her own fishhook. A youthful interest in nature matured into an undergraduate degree in biology. She left Jackson to pursue a career as a basic cancer researcher at the National Cancer Institute in Bethesda, MD. She was employed in one of the two laboratories that discovered the reverse transcriptase enzyme that plays a major role in many forms of cancer, and did early research on a cloned virus that was later to be named HIV. Following graduate courses in microbiology, she earned a graduate degree in Public Administration while working full-time in the laboratory. Her graduate work emphasized agricultural economics and the effects of introducing machinery to women farmers in Lesser Developed Countries. This was an outgrowth of her involvement in the 1970s international feminist movement. After 19 years in the laboratory, she moved into science administration managing grants and contracts, first for cancer research and then AIDS research. Nancy took early retirement in 1994. Her involvement in the local lesbian community includes a writers' group and several social groups.

Joan Cassidy, age 69, was born and raised in Forest Hills, New York. She holds a BA in English Literature and Journalism, and an MA in Journalism. She joined the Navy at age 22 and advanced quickly. She served for four years on active duty and 20 years in the Naval Reserve. She was one of the first women to command a reserve division and she retired as a Captain, at the highest rank a woman could then hold in the reserve. As a civilian, she worked for the Navy Department and when she took an early retirement she had moved up to Head of the Plans and Policy Department at the Naval Security Station. After retiring from the government, Joan founded Cassidy Associates and traveled around the USA presenting seminars in business writing. Currently she is totally retired and after attending an acting class, has appeared in several community theater productions including a portrayal of Big Mama in Tennessee Williams' *Cat on a Hot Tin Roof*.

Jacquelyn Gentry, age 60, was born in Dayton, and raised in Chattanooga, Tennessee. As Director of Public Interest Initiatives for the American Psychological Association (APA), Dr. Gentry coordinates APA-wide activities pertaining to violence, and works at the APA Office on AIDS. She directed the work of the APA Presidential Task Force on Violence and the Family as well as the development of a behavioral science research agenda on violence as part of the Human Capital Initiative. Before joining APA in 1989, Dr. Gentry worked for 22 years in the National Institute of Mental Health (NIMH) communications program. As Chief of the NIMH Science Communications, she directed a program to produce professional and public education materials on mental health. In addition to her career accomplishments, she loves to dance, swim, bicycle, tend her garden, and entertain for friends. In collaboration with her mother, she published a history of her family, tracing her roots back to Scottish immigrants in 1682. Currently she is writing a book about celebrating and honoring the wisdom and talents of old women.

DEFINING BEAUTY

The word "beauty" evokes different images for different people. But what does it mean to these three older lesbian women? Dr. Gentry recognizes that her definition is partially culture-bound, particularly in terms of personal appearance, such as the clothing she wears and how she presents herself. When she was younger, her view of beauty was more tied to mainstream social expectations and the way she viewed external beauty was much more centered around glamorous stereotypes. Now, her definition of external beauty is much broader; "it is no longer solely Atlantic City, Miss America beautiful." When she was younger she associated beauty with youth because of society's expectation of beauty as having youthful characteristics: energy, vitality, and sexiness. As an older lesbian, she tries to fight against this association. Now, she defines a person as beautiful in two ways: she can call someone's personality beautiful or she can look at a photograph of someone she has never met and judge their beauty solely by external appearance. A beautiful person may be someone with a craggy old face, gray hair, and a wizened appearance, a stunningly handsome preppy young man, or a beautiful young woman who fits many stereotypes. Judging external appearance is a very different way of defining beauty than calling someone she knows well beautiful. For example, when she calls a colleague or a friend beautiful, she may take into account their physical appearance, but also take in other important qualities such as their warmth, generosity, attitude, sense of humanity, and their ability to listen and to give, and to be in touch or to be engaged with her interests and topics she thinks are important. She can also call a celebrity like Hillary Clinton beautiful if she knows something about them, if the celebrity is involved in actions she thinks are important.

Ms. Brown believes beauty involves several components including physical and spiritual aspects. Her definition of beauty has basically not changed as she has aged; however, she finds that she is increasingly likely to reject mainstream beauty ideals. Ms. Brown was born when her mother was 40 and so she grew up with many older women present. In addition, her social activities revolved around church events which included spending much time with older women. Thus, her friends were mostly adults, not people her age. This influenced her beauty ideals; she has always thought older women were beautiful and in fact, in her teens, she had crushes on several white-haired women and was attracted to their physical appearance. They were generally tanned, with hair bleached by the Mississippi sun, but were not necessarily slim. She judges a woman's physical beauty by the way she dresses and carries herself. She also looks for an "aura of calmness, a look on the face or in the eyes that indicates an awareness of her self-confidence and appreciation for herself" which she is sensitive to detecting. Diction, intellect, and a good sense of humor are all central to her definition of beauty.

Ms. Cassidy's perception of beauty has changed over time. When she was 20, she would never look at a person with a white head of hair and think they were beautiful the way she does today. "I may have admired pretty white hair but it never would have occurred to me to be attracted to the woman under the white hair." She believes that expressions of "warmth, love, and softness" are beautiful. If these attributes, in addition to intellect, laughter, and a sense of humor, are present, a woman's physical appearance is not important to her. She pays attention to all of the senses when determining someone's beauty. For example, a beautiful person may have a delightful voice, a pleasant spice perfume scent, and feel soft and smooth. She believes that the mainstream ideals of beauty for women are ridiculously unattainable. When she sees fashion models, she thinks "who would want to look like that and who would want to wear those clothes?" It is very difficult for her not to be affected by these mainstream beauty norms and not to fantasize that one of these traditionally beautiful women would fall in love with her. She is so bombarded by these ideals that she cannot help but be affected by them yet she also works toward rejecting these ideals.

BEAUTY ROLE MODELS

Dr. Gentry's beauty role model on the most basic level is her mother. She has always admired her mother who had a great deal of energy, was generous and welcoming, kind, flexible, good-natured, had "a lot of vitality about her," was a community leader, was an excellent public speaker, was vitally engaged with others, was attractive, dressed nicely, and was smart and versatile. She admires the fact that her mother was able to work full-time and still be very active in community affairs. Now, at age 93, her mother has a lovely wrinkled face and white hair. Dr. Gentry's view of her mother is "a basic admiration for a beautiful person." However, as an adolescent, her beauty role models were more glamorous and were embodied by images of Hollywood movie stars in the 1950s. "Of all the movie idols, I believe that I wanted most of all to be like Esther Williams–a superb swimmer, surrounded by music and dance routines in the water, beautiful, and chased by the likes of Ricardo Montalban."

Ms. Brown's beauty role model is also her mother; "she was physically lovely. She was sweet, kind, gentle, genteel, a real 'southern belle.' She liked to entertain and welcomed people into her home with southern hospitality." An additional role model for Ms. Brown is Ingrid Bergman because of her physical appearance, her accent, and her talent. Julie Andrews is a third beauty role model due to her soprano voice. Her perception of male beauty is embodied by David Copperfield who possesses dark hair, strong features, and she appreciates men with a two-day shadow. Ms. Brown's beauty role models have not changed over time.

Ms. Cassidy's beauty role model growing up was Cary Grant. She wanted to look like him: tall, dark, and handsome and she wanted to be suave and debonair like him. Like Cary Grant, she wanted "to be able to smile at a woman and have her fall in her arms." She even practiced lighting her cigarette the way he did and imagined going though life wearing a tuxedo. Another beauty role model is Maureen Bunyon, a local news commentator who dresses beautifully and always looks tailored, composed, and lovely. "She was not too elaborate, just in extraordinarily good taste, and gave the impression that she was the kind of woman who could go anywhere and be welcome anywhere and always know which fork to use. She had a beautiful voice, a good brain, a sense of humor, and was very put together."

BEAUTY STANDARDS AND SELF-ESTEEM

The mainstream American beauty standard had varying impact on the three women interviewed. Dr. Gentry has always been fairly mainstream in her choice of clothes: she wears tailored clothes, with traditional designs, but she wears bright colors. She has stayed "pretty close to standards of dress of being in a professional role." When she came out as a lesbian she stopped wearing makeup. She has increased her admiration for "butch" looks and appearances which are more appealing to her now. She is annoyed with her wrinkles and by the fact that her body does not look as taut and fit as it used to and that she has lost her narrow waistline. She has never dyed her hair and believes it is graying "very nicely." She would never choose plastic surgery for herself because she sees it as too much of a hassle. However, she has never really been dissatisfied with her appearance. While overseeing the needs of her frail elderly parents, she has spent much time in nursing homes and has spent hours thinking about the aging process on the body and beauty, which is very humbling to her. She now appreciates the nice moments in life because she realizes more and more that it is indeed possible for her to become very sick or disabled. She has begun to be more accommodating to sickness and disability in herself and her friends and believes that attractiveness is unrelated to a person's disability. Growing older has not made her feel less beautiful. As she grows older, she has become more aware of beauty stereotypes and dismisses them. She respects and honors old people's experience and wisdom and therefore, counteracts ageism through a deliberate effort to tell people how old she is.

Ms. Brown has always felt like she could not engage in both the rough-and-tumble activities she so enjoyed and dress in the slim, skimpy dresses with high heels that mainstream culture emphasized. When buying clothes, she prefers comfort to fashion. This philosophy did not conflict with her work attire because as a scientist in a laboratory, trousers were the appropriate clothing. She would wear skirts and dresses only when she went out socially and to church. She was not aware of any lesbian communities until she was in her 20s so she was not concerned with what other lesbians would think of her dress. She identified more with the masculine aspects of others than with the feminine aspects and it was not until she reached age 30 or so that she allowed herself to be more feminine. She is now a "softer butch" than she once was. She thinks that this is due to a recognition of diversity in American society as a whole and in the lesbian community in particular. She feels more comfortable out of the closet and does not care so much what other people think of her. This is in contrast to when she was younger; then, "being gay was almost as bad as being a communist." She had gray hair until three years ago when she dyed her hair blond. Coloring her hair makes her feel better about herself and makes her look eight or ten years younger and fitter. In this aspect she acknowledges that she is caught up in the mainstream quest for youth. So, ideologically she rejects mainstream beauty ideals yet behaviorally still engages in some.

When Ms. Cassidy was younger, she wanted glamorous women to like her. When she entered the lesbian community, she felt required to declare herself a butch or a femme. So she identified herself with butch roles and did not wear pink clothes until several years ago. In fact, she felt more confined by lesbian beauty standards than by stereotypical mainstream ideals. She took part in the stereotypical beauty rituals (e.g., wearing high heels) to please her mother but not to attract women. As she has gotten older, staying within the confines of lesbian beauty standards is less important to her and she is now willing to look more feminine. For example, she looks good in pink and does indeed wear it. In addition, though there was a time when her friends would have made her feel uncomfortable for doing so, she currently has a body wave in her hair. As she ages, she is more willing to get in touch with her feminine side, and she buys soft, comfortable feminine pant suits, and engages in activities she has never done before (like her theater participation). Before her retirement, she had two wardrobes, one for the office including skirts and dresses, and one for leisure composed of trousers. Now, she is less likely to be influenced be other people to wear certain clothes and wears what she wants.

BEAUTY AND DATING

The three women interviewed noted that their choice of a partner has changed as they grow older. Though the presentation of a potential partner has been important to Dr. Gentry, personality has always been the deciding factor when choosing a partner. She does not need glamour in a partner, yet does prefer someone who takes pride in her or his appearance and dresses appropriately for an occasion. As she grows older, external appearance has decreased in importance.

When choosing a partner, Ms. Brown looks for "a package." She makes a mental list of positive and negative attributes of a potential date. The positive must outweigh the negative aspects of a potential date for Ms. Brown to ask her out. She presents herself as tailored and comfortable, and looks for a feminine appearance in her partner.

Ms. Cassidy's choice of partner has changed as she has grown older. When she was younger, she would not have searched for signs of intellect the way she does now. This change grew from experience: she knew some stereotypically beautiful women and was disappointed in their character. Now, just being able to look at someone who is beautiful is not enough. The shell (the outer appearance) is not what is going to make a relationship last in the long run, nor keep her interested. She is increasingly selective in what she wants a partner to be like. While she still is attracted to beautiful women, she now strives to find out more about who is inside the beautiful shell before dating.

For example, Ms. Cassidy needs to know that a potential partner can take care of herself and is socially at-ease around other people.

Ms. Brown suggests that the recognition of ageism in the lesbian community is imperative. Compassion towards the experiences of older women and their specific needs is warranted. What are lesbian women going to do to take care of themselves and each other as they get older and less healthy? Lesbian communities need to address this important social and political question.

CONCLUSION

The three women interviewed presented ideas of beauty that, while individual and unique, nonetheless have common threads. All agree that their definition of beauty has expanded as they have aged and that they are increasingly likely to reject mainstream beauty ideals. All three emphasize that there are multiple levels of beauty. Two women report that mothers are beauty role models and two report that their beauty role models have not changed much as they have aged. Yet they also present such varying personas as Esther Williams, Julie Andrews, David Copperfield, Cary Grant, and Maureen Bunyon as role models. All report that their beauty standards have changed as they age and they feel freer to dress how they choose to instead of how they are expected to dress. For Dr. Gentry this change means becoming more "butch" and for the other two this change means becoming more feminine. Finally, all three women's choice of partner has changed as they have aged, with two saying that their partner's external appearance has decreased in importance. Thus, as these lesbians have aged, they have broadened their definition of beauty, their choice of partner and style of dressing, and have become increasingly active in rejecting mainstream beauty standards.

Beauty on the Borderland:
On Being Black Lesbian and Beautiful

Jennifer Lyle
Jeanell Jones
Gail Drakes

SUMMARY. Everyday identities are constructed and re-constructed. For persons with multiple identities as women, as Black, as queer, as budding scholars, etc., the conceptions they have of beauty and of attractiveness are colored by the identities they create and maintain. In this piece, three graduate students of color share their experiences and per-

Jennifer Lyle is a doctoral student in the Social Work and Sociology joint program at the University of Michigan. Her research focuses on welfare, women's reproduction, and pregnancy policy in the United States. She is active in welfare rights, organizing locally in Michigan and nationally. She is also active in organizing the people of color queer communities in the Midwest region.

Jeanell Jones is a 23-year-old West-Indian American, bisexual woman. She is in her fourth year Psychology doctoral program and first year master's in Public Policy program at the University of Michigan. Her research examines the relationship between attitudes toward refugee and immigrant communities and the public policies that shape their lives. In her spare time she enjoys reading, writing poetry and fiction, and swimming in the blue waters of the Atlantic (on the Caribbean side, of course).

Gail Drakes is a 24-year-old Black bisexual woman from Hartford, Connecticut. Her graduate research in history focuses on representations of African-American history on film; therefore, she spends a great deal of time thinking about the power of the image and how those images are increasingly relevant to understanding how we all perceive beauty, in theory and in practice.

Address correspondence for Jennifer, Jeanell, and Gail to: University of Michigan, SSW, 1080 South University, Room 1794A, Ann Arbor, MI 48109-1106.

[Haworth co-indexing entry note]: "Beauty on the Borderland: On Being Black Lesbian and Beautiful." Lyle, Jennifer, Jeanell Jones, and Gail Drakes. Co-published simultaneously in *Journal of Lesbian Studies* (The Haworth Press, Inc.) Vol. 3, No. 4, 1999, pp. 45-53; and: *Lesbians, Levis and Lipstick: The Meaning of Beauty in Our Lives* (ed: Jeanine C. Cogan and Joanie M. Erickson) The Haworth Press, Inc., 1999, pp. 45-53; and: *Lesbians, Levis and Lipstick: The Meaning of Beauty in Our Lives* (ed: Jeanine C. Cogan and Joanie M. Erickson) Harrington Park Press, an imprint of The Haworth Press, Inc., 1999, pp. 45-53. Single or multiple copies of this article are available for a fee from The Haworth Document Delivery Service [1-800-342-9678, 9:00 a.m. - 5:00 p.m. (EST). E-mail address: getinfo@haworthpressinc.com].

45

spectives on the topic of lesbian beauty. Through their dialogue they examine the functions of beauty in their communities, what attractiveness means for them as women, as Black women and as Black lesbians, and the power of images in their everyday lives. In their conversations, we see how three Black women, in their attempt to remain unfettered, must navigate their way through many social roles. *[Article copies available for a fee from The Haworth Document Delivery Service: 1-800-342-9678. E-mail address: getinfo@haworthpressinc.com]*

Every Friday night we gather in the back of the Student Union: lesbian and bisexual women of color. In this weekly support group we share ideas, vent about the week's frustrations, and relish in the comfort of other women traversing the crossroads. In this space our racial identities, our gender identities, and our sexual identities have found a home–here we can be female, of color, lesbian and everything in between. One week, one of the women mentions that she would like to write a collaborative article on lesbian beauty. A few weeks later three of us are in her apartment discussing the topic.

We represent an interesting collage of Black women. Jennifer, who identifies as lesbian, grew up in Denver, Colorado, but came of age in the San Francisco/Bay Area. Jeanell has only been living in the United States, and mainly in the Midwest, for a few years, having been brought up in the Caribbean. She identifies herself as bisexual. And the other sister, Gail, is a second-generation Caribbean-American from the East Coast. She identifies herself as a butch bisexual woman. From different coasts, different countries, and different identifications within the lesbian community we sit on common terrain and try to tackle the huge and amorphous topic of Black lesbian beauty.

BEAUTY AS IDENTIFICATION: I AM A LESBIAN DAMMIT–SO FLIRT WITH ME!

In-group identification has many positive functions. Being identified as a Black lesbian by other Black lesbians sometimes serves to create solidarity. This solidarity is meaningful because of how it sometimes functions to diminish isolation and alienation felt by Black lesbians living in a population where they may feel they are not part of the majority. It also distinguishes you as a potential partner. In the end, women try to 'look lesbian' or not for different reasons, but these reasons are not without consequences. Being visible as a lesbian can have positive and negative political and/or social consequences and depends very much on context and whether an individual is encouraged or discouraged to express herself.

In this discussion we questioned how beauty images are interpreted and if we create a place within, outside of or despite of those images. We also discussed in what context being identified becomes an important issue.

Jennifer: In the Bay Area what's beautiful exemplifies that you are a Black woman and lesbian. The lesbians I know don't wear make-up; they wear their hair short and natural. They're not necessarily about sexualizing their form; their stature and their clothes are pretty functional. To look this way is popular and safe.

Gail: Because . . .

Jennifer: Because it's the Oakland/San Francisco Bay Area, where it's clear there is a different kind of a viewpoint. Different from Ann Arbor where it's difficult to identify queer women. I think that this is because in Ann Arbor it is not as safe to represent your femaleness as you see fit. While living in Oakland I didn't really worry about the consequences of not "looking feminine." I didn't feel that I had to follow certain structures. My idea of Black lesbian beauty was formed in the context of coming out . . . being in California in a very supportive environment where *I* was encouraged to define my beauty. Here it is much different, especially how people interact with you. In the Black community . . . I feel that regardless of where I am I "dress" for Black folks, especially if I don't know them. . . . Often times here I feel less accepted by the Black community because of the way I look, so I make sure that I look presentable. It's important for me not to feel alienated from the Black community. In this new context I am being reformed–reforming my perceptions of myself somewhat based on my reception here. One cannot help but internalize the messages and pressures to "fit" or be "acceptable." This constant feeling of outsiderness wears on me at times.

Gail: That's true. Also, the look among Black lesbians or bisexuals (or other queer women of color) can be very different, even within the same geographical area. All of this makes me think about the ways in which the idea of beauty in queer communities functions not only as beauty for beauty's sake, but beauty–or specifically fashion–as identification as part of the queer community. I don't have the time, nor am I particularly inclined, to go out of my way to look a certain way to fit some image–did someone say stereotype?–of what a queer woman should look like. But at the same time I've got to admit that it is truly frustrating to see another woman who is identifiably queer and she's attractive and instead of figuring out if I'm going to find the guts to flirt a little I've got to deal with the fact that she's not "identifying me back." For all she knows, I could be some homophobe who's staring at her because she looks different! I believe in being "out," but I've never thought that style of dress should be the only defining action. But then, not only politically, but also personally I would like to be identified as queer. But how do I do that in a way that is true to how I see myself? I feel like striking that balance is difficult, I want folks to "know the deal"; if only to avoid the whole drawn-out "coming-out moment" with acquaintances! But then I think that there is something wrong with me going out to buy some lesbian "look."

Jeanell: That's funny, you have group pressure so that you can have solidarity. And also personal pressures so that you can get a date.

Gail: The latter is more of an issue for me these days! When you add to this mix an identification as bisexual, well, it gets complicated! There's no bisexual "look" that I'm aware of. . . . Which is just as well. I think that there's an identification issue that is relevant, but then, can't that go too far? Don't some of the attempts at being identifiably queer run the risk of crossing the line and limiting what's viewed as beautiful?

Jeanell: I don't have a set image, style or manner of dress. I never thought about having a look, it's whatever I feel like wearing. What I'm attracted to is a person who prescribes her own look.

Jennifer: That's interesting that you say that. You wouldn't say that you see yourself on any side . . . closer to any side . . .

Jeanell: On the butch/femme continuum?

Jennifer: Like my experiences since I've been here; people are confused because they don't know where to put me. They'll be shocked that I'm wearing a dress. They don't know where to place me because I guess my look seems inconsistent to them. I'm sure that the fact that I have a mustache and beard and I let it grow really throws them off. I've had a different education about how I can present myself. I feel like despite social pressure to appear certain ways, I've been allowed to express myself how I've wanted. Certain things that I wear are on different sides of the continuum in terms of gender-ized clothing. I'm just curious, do you feel you or your clothing is more indicative of one gender identification or another?

Jeanell: If I do put on a pair of jeans I'll often put on a pair of high heel boots. That kind of throws it off for people . . . the look is not complete.

Gail: Those items that strike that balance seem to be a big issue in the fashion industry. Several seasons ago wearing men's clothing was fashion-able, jackets especially. In teen magazines they were referred to as "the boyfriend jacket." There was this whole little imaginary story line that the girl was borrowing this jacket from her boyfriend. The rationalization of this blurring of the gender lines in fashion continues. Recently, I had a trial subscription to one of your major American women's fashion magazines. This magazine warns constantly against the dangers of looking "severe" and the need to "accentuate your femininity" by wearing a lingerie top under your suit or a pair of stiletto heels. What was quite funny to me was that in the middle of all this there was a photo of Marlene Dietrich wearing this *fierce* gray suit, *without* the teddy underneath. We all knew that it wasn't her boyfriend's jacket.

Jeanell: I think a lot of it has to do with what you're socialized to believe you're supposed to come out of the house in. In the Bahamas if you're wearing bright, radiant colored clothing no one will look at you twice because you're matching the scenery. On the other hand if you're a woman wearing army fatigues people will look at you and wonder what you're going through. You would have to sex it up a little.

Jennifer: Staying within the cultural bounds of staying sexy and womanly.

Jeanell: I think anything that I find comfortable I adapt to. I never thought about clothing being self-defining or sexually defining. I never thought about image, or having the perfect image to go along with the setting. When you talk about different norms and different places shaping how you dress and what you find acceptable . . . I've been in some weird places, between Wisconsin and Ann Arbor, I've struggled not to let myself and my sense of beauty become ruled by the spirit of these places. In terms of the lesbian culture of Wisconsin, if you were White, female and gay, Madison was the place to be. All you had to have was a flannel-shirt, jeans and boots. That was the look. But that look wasn't necessarily the look I wanted. Not because it was something that identified me as lesbian but because it was like having a uniform. For me this made it more difficult to find someone attractive.

ATTRACTIVENESS: WELCOME TO MY QUEENDOM

Though standards of beauty and attractiveness have changed over the years, what has remained constant for us is being excluded from this 'standard.' As Black women, and as women who identify as bisexual or lesbian, to exist outside of current standards of beauty has been both frustrating and enriching. This experience has allowed us to expand our notions of beauty while challenging the standards of the respective communities in which we live.

Jennifer: Before I got my hair cut people had a hard time identifying me as a lesbian. I was worried that if I cut my hair people are going to think I'm a lesbian because I have short hair. When I did cut my hair short I thought, finally, people are going to understand that I am a lesbian. So, I have a question for you Gail. Did you go through any of this drama in your hair process?

Gail: You know not to get me started on the hair! Because it's been quite the hair adventure.

Jennifer: Well, it's a big beauty thing for us colored girls. It's tied to many constructs of rating and measuring our beauty.

Gail: Definitely. I'm teaching a class in African American Studies this semester and the subject this past week has been hair, Black hair, and Madam

C.J. Walker. I wanted students to talk about Madam Walker, her ideas and how she was criticized by leaders like Booker T. Washington who felt that straightened hair did not affirm Black women's beauty. I also wanted them to see the story of Black hair as a continuing one. Most of the students in this course are Black, and all of them have hair! So I was hoping that they would make connections. It was really interesting. There were two things that were the most striking for me. The first was how strongly many of the women in the course saw hair–straight hair–as a critical part of what they thought was beautiful. Beyond that, straight hair was not beautiful all by itself: you had to style it right. If you don't have straight hair, you are kind of "out of the game." This wasn't the first time I've heard ideas like this, and it wasn't the first time I've countered them, but it was the first time I've critiqued these kinds of ideas with a head full of short, nappy hair. I could just feel the way in which my words were being read differently than when my hair was straight. I was concerned about not coming on too strong, and the students were concerned about not offending me–the woman with the grade book–with their claims about their unalienable right to a relaxer.

For me, cutting my hair–an idea that started off really simply, and pretty non-political–has become more about asserting and defining beauty as a Black woman, as well as a queer woman. Cutting my hair just to identify as queer . . . well, I have the same issue as dressing to suit that purpose; it doesn't feel right. There is a poem that I love by a Black Caribbean Canadian dyke that talks about a dyke getting locks instead of keeping her short clipped style because the other dykes are not taking her seriously with "just a fro" on her head. The poem argues a point that's an important one for me. It questions some unwritten "rules" of what's acceptable beauty in white and people of color communities.

Recently a Black male colleague of mine offered an interesting spin; he thought my hair was great, but he went out of his way to mention that he wouldn't want his girlfriend to try it. I thought that was very interesting . . . Was he afraid people would get the wrong idea? But as for being identified as gay, I haven't really noticed too much of that yet. I think that although the Black female students here tend to wear their hair long and straightened, for the most part, there is this increased acceptance of natural hair on some levels. Although there is an entire portion of the beauty business that is going to make sure that we are surrounded with images of relaxed hair, some natural styles have popped up in Black women's magazines. So politically now it's uncool to assume someone's gay because they wear their hair natural. It seems like I'm going to have to go back to queer buttons and T-shirts and such.

Jeanell: Do you think that it has anything to do with the body? I have a friend who is always identified as a lesbian or butch because of the way she walks and talks. Therefore, if you're muscular or carry yourself assertively you must be a lesbian. What are they saying? When we talk about butch/ femme why do looks and size have to be key distinctions?

Jennifer: Also true is that often people will refer to a woman they perceive as unattractive by saying that she looks like a dyke or he-she. If she doesn't fit some common beauty standards she may be referred to in those terms. As women, the expectation is that we would do anything to prevent being considered ugly; unless you're a lesbian. To be a lesbian is to be outside the realm of beauty. To avoid being seen as ugly or lesbian we are expected to torture ourselves to meet impossible standards of beauty.

Jeanell: If we don't do these things we are not attractive to men.

Jennifer: That's a serious thought that I had about myself. Initially when I cut my hair and let my facial hair alone I was worried about my attractiveness. Then I felt freed up because my focus was not on enticing men or appealing to men. It took me some time to understand how that affected my perception of myself.

Jeanell: When you look at images and if you dissect images there's definitely something out there for heterosexual women and what that should look like. In terms of lesbians it's less clear.

Jennifer: How do we imagine ourselves as beautiful?

Jeanell: When Jennifer said 'imagining ourselves as beautiful' that just rang a bell. In Toni Morrison's book, *The Bluest Eye*, we see a Black girl trying to envision herself as beautiful, hoping that she can fit the right images. But in reality what is true beauty? There are a lot of these images of what the good looking butch or femme looks like. It's always a white woman.

One of the things that affects the way I think about beauty is my growing up in the Bahamas. As children we were taught that true beauty resides in the face. "If yinna have pretty face, all da rest will do." The idea behind this saying was that true beauty was what you were born with, a kind of essentialized, natural beauty. If you were over or underweight you could exercise or eat. All of these issues were fixable, but without a pretty face there was no salvation.

My search for a woman with a pretty face could lead me to a dyke with a motorcycle and a leather jacket or a dyke with dreads down her back and hemp woven dress. My messages from home and the acceptance of nontraditional modes of beauty in the lesbian community work together to allow me the freedom to find an attractive mate and be found attractive by a mate without popular fashion magazines *coloring* my choices.

What I think is beautiful, is the aura you radiate. What's interesting to me is we're assuming the image is what's going to make us attractive to someone and I'm not sure that's what I go for. Anyone can put together an image. Right now in Black culture we're going through a whole change of trying to look more afrocentric–an interesting trend is emerging. What we identify as a Black lesbian is often a person who wears her hair natural, uses no make-up, and wears "dreads." I wonder how those images are now regarded; if it's gonna make straight Black folk think they might be misidentified as queer (chuckle).

DEFINING THE TERRAIN OF BLACK LESBIAN BEAUTY

As the model in Figure 1 represents, trying to find images of, and standards for, Black lesbian beauty may be akin to searching for a needle in a haystack. Ascertaining what it means to be a beautiful Black lesbian and how contemporary images of beauty fit together is tricky terrain. For one, popular images represent beautiful female bodies as tall, White, extremely thin, and virtually curve-less (this is represented by oval 1), something that by definition (and biology!) excludes Black women. The intersection of ovals 1 and 2 represents the images of Black women as both (1) slightly darker painted versions of their White sisters, with European facial features: narrow nose, light skin color and straight hair, and body types and, (2) the exotic, sexually available, African women off the pages of National Geographic. In between these most common portrayals of Black female beauty is how the majority of Black women (beautiful but under-appreciated) really look, which is represented by oval 2. The third oval represents images of lesbian beauty though while rare, also fall prey to the definitions produced by the fashion industry. The intersection of 1 and 3 represents the queer woman who graces the pages of a gay magazine as a strong, slightly butch, White female. When Black women are portrayed in these magazines, poised on the arm of or behind the White model, they become the fashion accessories of White dykes. This is represented by the tiny intersection of ovals 1, 2 and 3.

From this model and our conversation, we clearly feel there are significant

FIGURE 1. Defining the Terrain of Black Lesbian Beauty

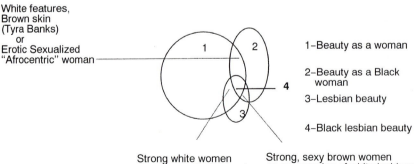

White features,
Brown skin
(Tyra Banks)
    or
Erotic Sexualized
"Afrocentric" woman

1–Beauty as a woman

2–Beauty as a Black woman

3–Lesbian beauty

4–Black lesbian beauty

Strong white women
(i.e., female firefighters)

Strong, sexy brown women
as accessories of white lesbians

limitations to what is considered beautiful. There exists a socially asserted standard and some subcategories–where those who don't quite make the standard exist. These outside definitions have so arranged our experiences and conceptions of beauty, that at times realizing and embracing positive and affirming notions of our beauty has been somewhat difficult. We have found as bisexual and lesbian women we have been allowed greater freedom in determining our beauty. However, as women of African descent, even within the lesbian community, self-defining is not limitless. As we continue to expand the too-narrow view of beauty we expect that beauty will be used to describe the broad range of attributes with which people come into this world.

Doing Beauty:
Negotiating Lesbian Looks
in Everyday Life

Tania N. Hammidi
Susan B. Kaiser

SUMMARY. Beauty is often formulated as a singular image, system, or narrative. Missing in these formulations are conceptualizations of personal desire, agency, and affiliation with community aesthetics. The following essay seeks to "complicate" current understandings of beauty–understandings that implicitly assume heterosexuality–by focusing on how lesbians *do* beauty to negotiate within and across four discourses. These discourses, we argue, function like cultural conversations that include verbal and visual messages, individual acts and media images, and dominant and community looks. Lesbians negotiate mixed responses to these discourses, in part, through lesbian styling. In the process, lesbians' assertions of agency allow for a reclaiming of beauty. To illustrate the ways lesbians re-frame and reclaim beauty in everyday life, we rely upon the voices and experiences of lesbians from Northern California. *[Article copies available for a fee from The Haworth Document Delivery Service: 1-800-342-9678. E-mail address: getinfo@haworthpressinc. com]*

Tania N. Hammidi has recently completed a Master of Science degree in Community Development at the University of California, Davis.

Susan B. Kaiser is Professor of Textiles and Clothing, and Women and Gender Studies, and Director of the Science and Society Program at the University of California, Davis.

Address correspondence to: Dr. Susan Kaiser, Division of Textiles and Clothing, University of California, Davis, CA 95616 (E-mail: sbkaiser@ucdavis.edu).

[Haworth co-indexing entry note]: "Doing Beauty: Negotiating Lesbian Looks in Everyday Life." Hammidi, Tania N., and Susan B. Kaiser. Co-published simultaneously in *Journal of Lesbian Studies* (The Haworth Press, Inc.) Vol. 3, No. 4, 1999, pp. 55-63; and: *Lesbians, Levis and Lipstick: The Meaning of Beauty in Our Lives* (ed: Jeanine C. Cogan and Joanie M. Erickson) The Haworth Press, Inc., 1999, pp. 55-63; and: *Lesbians, Levis and Lipstick: The Meaning of Beauty in Our Lives* (ed: Jeanine C. Cogan and Joanie M. Erickson) Harrington Park Press, an imprint of The Haworth Press, Inc., 1999, pp. 55-63. Single or multiple copies of this article are available for a fee from The Haworth Document Delivery Service [1-800-342-9678, 9:00 a.m. - 5:00 p.m. (EST). E-mail address: getinfo@haworthpressinc.com].

55

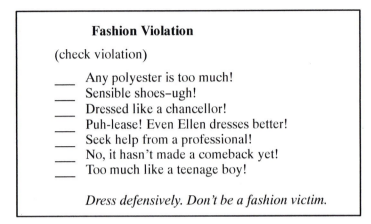

The above citation, issued by the Fashion Police during a break at a gay, lesbian, bisexual and transgender community awards ceremony, is meant to poke fun at how gays and lesbians *style*. These citations overemphasize certain details and symbols in a playful and self-effacing manner, but the game becomes one-sided, focusing unduly on lesbian looks. Lesbians have long been accused, by straights, gay men, and lesbians alike, of knowing neither how to dress nor how to participate appropriately in the realms of beauty and aesthetics. Lesbian looks are stereotyped as outdated; aesthetically naive; too political, practical, and dull; and divested from traditional feminine beauty. In this context, lesbian beauty is in danger of being perceived as an oxymoron.

In this essay, we assume that there is more to beauty than prescribed, normative standards of beauty, femininity, and consumer culture. We open a space for conceptualizing beauty in the context of lesbians' visual negotiations of meaning in everyday life. In so doing, the breadth of "beauties" celebrating lesbian identities and pride becomes clear. First, we argue that the roots of cultural stereotypes about lesbian looks can be understood in the context of problematic assumptions underlying how people *see* and conceptualize female beauty: as an image, a system, or a narrative. We outline our understandings of these framings, and then suggest an alternative strategy of conceptualizing–one that acknowledges beauty as something lesbians (and women in general) *do* in everyday life: negotiate competing and contradictory discourses that operate within and beyond lesbian communities. We use the term "discourse" to mean a cultural conversation that works through ideas, images, contradictions, and ambivalences. This conversation includes visual and verbal messages, individual acts and media images, dominant and lesbian looks, and so on. Managing appearance in everyday life, then, becomes a political and aesthetic act of visually negotiating these diverse cultural conversations.

In the second part of the paper, we discuss what it means to *do* beauty according to four different discourses: dominant lesbian beauty, inner beauty, dominant beauty, and political beauty. We identified these discourses through an iterative process, moving between existing conceptualizations and critiques of beauty, and lesbians' testimonies on appearance-related issues. Our need to "unframe frameworks" (Olesen, 1994, p. 160) is consistent with many other current feminist projects that aim to decenter and diversify understandings of women's lives. Because we see beauty as something lesbians do in both shared and individualized ways, in relation and resistance to diverse discourses, we supplement our analysis with the voices and experiences of lesbians interviewed in Northern California for a larger study of identity, community, and lesbian appearance styles (Freitas, Kaiser, & Hammidi, 1996).[1]

SEEING BEAUTY

By what standards are lesbians considered to be beautiful, and by whom? In this section, we suggest three ways in which female beauty has traditionally been conceptualized. We complicate the assumption that beauty is exclusively an image, a system, or a narrative. Indeed, opening up the boundaries around each of these concepts is necessary as we begin to explore the place of beauty in lesbians' lives.

Beauty as Image. Typically, beauty has been defined as an image. This beauty-as-image assumption emphasizes the *look* itself, prioritizing the visual product over the process of managing appearance. Moreover, the look becomes framed as an ideal that appears to be static–one look, an accumulation of visual successes which add up to a whole and complete "beautiful" image: white, feminine, thin, young (usually very young), fashionable, upper-middle class, long-haired, and filled with heterosexual promise.

Secondly, the beauty-as-image assumption locates individuals and groups as haves and have-nots. The image of those who "have" beauty (i.e., airbrushed, thin, white, and so on) is a highly problematic one. It does not explain contextual and community variations, interpersonal relationships, pleasures, or desires. This concept also fails to acknowledge the active and strategic negotiations that are so crucial to the looks women construct and interpret in everyday life. Finally, the singular image concept implies the need for a singular system.

Beauty as System. This approach deals with the idea of beauty as a system, where cultural practices for femininity are fundamental to the arrangement between females and males:

There is no other cultural complex in modern society which touches upon individual behavior that is as rigorously conceived and executed, total, and minutely policed by collective observation and moral authority than are feminine beauty standards. (MacCannell & MacCannell, 1987, p. 208)

Simone de Beauvoir (1952) suggests that the beauty system reflects the "unfinished business" of being a woman whose work is never done. While a beauty-as-system approach does complicate the role beauty plays in women's lives, it implicitly places beauty in the realm of heterosexual attraction. Given that systems have boundaries, this approach tends to promote a kind of binary ("in" or "out") thinking. Feminist critiques drawing on a systems approach exemplify this binary thinking: those who are in the system suffer from a false consciousness, duped by the media and/or capitalism. Those who are outside of the system are not feminine. In this formulation, all lesbians who do not subscribe to traditional femininity become relegated to this outside position. In contrast, lesbians who use the tools of traditional femininity (for example, femmes) in their appearance styling, are duped because they are in the system. The system concept also promotes the assumption that there can be a "natural" look, which is masculine. Presumably, men have this look, as do women outside of the feminine beauty system. What follows is only a false choice: reinforce the dominance (naturalness) of the male norm or participate in the (un-natural) beauty system.

Beauty as Narrative. Like the systems approach, a beauty-as-narrative assumption views beauty as a major component of the arrangement between the sexes. Whereas a systems approach places more emphasis on male-female relations within cultural capitalism, a narrative approach generates a cultural script with a "live happily ever after" quality. Naomi Wolf (1991) talks about beauty as a myth, with a story line or narrative structure that serves to keep women in their place. That is, beauty objectively and universally exists. Women must want it in themselves, and men must want it in women. Beauty is imperative for women, but not for men. As the story goes, the beauty myth is based on sexual selection, associating beauty to women's fertility. Obviously, this story doesn't work too well for lesbian beauty, since the purpose is not to lure the best male. Further, the story line does not allow for more than one script; it cannot explain diverse looks, changes in looks, or pleasures outside of the dominant cultural script.

DOING BEAUTY

We are specifically concerned that the image, system, and narrative assumptions offer little to account for lesbians' abilities to re-frame and reclaim beauty, as individuals, couples, small friendship circles, or communities. Yet we agree with the fundamental contradiction that MacCannell and MacCannell (1987) and Tseëlon (1995) highlight: that dominant culture asks women to accept their own "fundamental ugliness" in the process of caring about beauty. This contradiction is especially acute for lesbians, who may need to reconcile dominant and diverse community expectations. We see *doing beauty* as a process of visually articulating and negotiating cultural contradictions and personal ambivalences (i.e., conflicting emotions).

We submit that a negotiation-of-discourses approach allows more agency than can be offered by singular stereotypes, bounded systems, or cultural narratives, because such an approach emphasizes not only cultural and community forces, but also personal emotions and actions. Following are brief sketches of four beauty discourses through which lesbians work, differently, to understand and achieve beauty. We offer these discourses as non-uniform aesthetic camps–each with their own visual logic and ethical issues–to which lesbians share a variety of responses: from vulnerability to ambivalence to resistance, from community pride to political refusal. Hence, as the contexts, communities, and role of the women negotiating these discourses change, the aesthetics each camp offers shift in appeal and importance.

Dominant Lesbian Beauty. As individuals and lesbian communities assert strength and agency, their codes gain potency as markers of lesbian existence. Part of this assertion may entail the process of expressing queer identities. Whether or not individual lesbians strive to express queer identities, aesthetic preferences vary as greatly as their choosers do. Aesthetic codes from urban, rural, punk, ethnic, femme, butch, professional, transsexual and political lesbian communities all offer different and overlapping aesthetic cues to mark women as beautiful, lesbian, or queer. Aesthetic choices are explained in terms of freedom within the lesbian community; in fact, community freedom emerges as a key tenant of lesbian style and beauty by self-identified lesbians:

> "Anything goes." (White, 23 years)
> "I love (being) around people who have done a lot of really amazing things with their looks." (African American, 27)
> "Comfort is the name of the game." (White, 28)

Yet, in an ironic twist of this freedom, many lesbians report pressures within their communities to ascribe to particular queer codes. The image of "looking butch" has loomed as the primary marker of lesbian visibility within both gay and straight stereotypical images. Diverse lesbian communities offer up their own versions of the most beautiful dyke–based on racial, geographic, and class-originated aesthetics. Yet the dominant aesthetic codes of "looking butch" are ones against which lesbians are most strongly evaluated as being either queer or not. Thus, marking one's queerness in a way that is on par with dominant standards not only visually legitimizes a woman's queerness, but also "ups the ante" of her beautiful appeal. Appearance choices that fall outside of this dominant lesbian aesthetic–make-up, long hair, fashionable feminine clothing, and dresses, for example–rank lower on the beauty scale, simply because of their unrecognizability as cues of lesbian existence.

As a 27-year-old South Asian dyke reports: "I just had an argument last week with a lesbian about the fact that, excuse me, but I don't have to have short hair to be a dyke. Okay? You know, I'm not going to cut my hair to be a dyke." Her dignity in recognizing that her homosexuality does not have to be clad in a flat-top speaks to a key tenet of many long-haired, feminine lesbians who, in the words of JoAnn Loulan (1992, in Everett & Christopher), have been "outlawed from the lesbian community" at various times. One European-American lesbian, 26, echoes this sentiment, "I don't wear my dresses to lesbian bars. Dykes don't approve."

Likewise, while the dominant lesbian beauty discourse promotes masculine style, it also clearly devalues cultural styles that cannot be read as chic or urban. For example, as one woman mockingly states: "They have big hair in Walnut Creek. I think they have a sort of Latina influence, you know–how they spray their hair up really high, and it is a very elaborate frontal hair do and long in the back." The race- and class-based biases here are also evident in the middle-class, masculine chic, urban butch symbol of lesbian beauty. This symbol is steeped in race and class privilege that uses visibility as a marker of both credibility and beauty.

Inner Beauty. The parameters of achieving ultimate inner beauty are not based on visibility or visual cues, but are based on principles of empowerment. The inner beauty discourse, in fact, is popular because of its attempt to avoid discrimination on the basis of how a person looks. Anti-materialist at its core, this discourse is similar to many spiritual, maternal, and political philosophies that seek to center identity and to cultivate psychic, rather than consumer, goods. For example, a 27-year-old African American woman describes: "I would walk 7 or 8 miles a day and go there and there and anywhere I wanted to . . . I felt strong. I didn't have to depend on anybody." Her feelings of physical strength and independence are clearly part of her own empowerment. Linking physical strength to mental strength seems a likely leap, considering how dominant beauty myths appear to reinforce docile femininity rather than bodily or mental strength.

Many lesbians described that they are drawn to women who express their inner beauty by seeming to be visually "at home" in their bodies. A 46-year-old Dutch-Portuguese American woman notes: "I think a body is really powerful when a person is comfortable in her own skin. You can just tell people who are really comfortable with their body." This feeling of "comfort" can be expressed in many ways. One woman describes it in terms of her self-confidence, noting that appreciating who she is allows her to deflect homophobia: "I . . . feel . . . somewhat powerful and am not intimidated by people glaring."

While this feeling does empower many women, the inner beauty discourse that focuses on feeling comfortable with one's given body and working on inner strengths rather than outer beauty, trivializes the importance appearance plays in both identity and visual communication. Adornment or concern with appearance has no place in the inner beauty aesthetic. Lesbians who "do beauty" that involves plastic surgery or transgendered concerns with the body find no support in the inner beauty discourse. Hence, women may experience this discourse as one that induces guilt rather than a feeling of strength.

Dominant Beauty. The dominant beauty discourse conflates fashion with beauty, so that the most beautiful is also the most fashionable. The upper-middle-class markings are clear, as are other "fashionable" prerequisites of femininity–thin, white, elegant, young, heterosexual. These qualities become standards against which all women are measured. A male-to-female trans-sexual lesbian, for whom the feminine ideal provides a strategic model for passing as female without exposure, articulated her investments in resembling the ideal. Her "clodhopper feet" and lack of training "by *Cosmopolitan* magazine and other magazines about how to be a girl" become recognized sites of negotiating her transsexual identity.

As more lesbian models and stars appear in dominant media, homosexuality is articulated only along the lines of dominant beauty standards. Lesbians express clear awareness of this whitewashing effect, with varying degrees of concern. One woman takes an adamant stand against this image of lesbians, accusing it of marking another erasure of homosexuality: "Somebody came bowling in a straight-woman-shorts-set ensemble and we all rolled our eyeballs. She wasn't dressed like a dyke at all. She dressed like a straight woman." Others offer less of a hard line, expressing pleasure in the "innovation and creativity" of the fashion world and the clothing it has to offer. Thus, lesbians report varying degrees of vulnerability to these standards, at different times in their lives.

Political Beauty. A woman's right to conceive of her own appearance and bodily characteristics–hairy or hairless, bearded or plucked, breasted or reduced/enlarged, high or flat heeled–become highly contested choices in the control over lesbians' beauty. Second-wave feminists of the late 1960s and early 1970s often framed choices in this either-or manner to counter the emphasis of normative beauty standards on women's femininity and marketability. Evans and Thorton (1989) describe how this second wave feminist "experiment" with the "natural" look aimed to renegotiate new categories of beauty. Many lesbians in our conversations reported contending with these concerns.

Psychological and physical comfort becomes a primary criterion in political beauty discourse, and lesbians articulate this criterion relative to clothing choices from shoes to bras to textures. Both a Puerto-Rican non-bra wearer who "hate[s] to feel clamped" and a European American sports-shoe wearer who says "I want to feel that I can move freely in whatever I am wearing" express a fair degree of freedom with these choices within their lesbian communities. However, lesbians must also negotiate desire (see Chapkis, 1986), and the clothing styles associated with feminine desire may seem to stand in direct opposition to dominant feminist positions. For example, one lesbian expresses feeling constrained by her lesbian political community: "I don't feel comfortable going to bars in a miniskirt or going out in tights or something . . . even though they are incredibly comfortable." Here, the political notion of "comfort" shows its biases around issues of beauty and women's agency within the beauty system.

CONCLUSION

Prevailing assumptions about beauty lead us to "see" it as an image (whose image?), a system (who is in it, and who is not?), or a narrative (whose story is told?). These assumptions become especially problematic for lesbians, who are excluded according to prevailing stereotypes about how lesbians look and what they value (does a concern for fashion or beauty mean that a woman isn't "really" gay?). Yet stereotypical challenges operate within the lesbian community: If the most beautiful lesbian is woman-born, white, masculine, middle class, thin, and chic, then who gets left out of this formula, and at what cost? Whose "policing" wins out in the struggle for self-determination and lesbians' reclamations of sexuality, body, and spirit?

As we begin to see beauty as a negotiation of existing and emerging discourses, we will see many more "beauties" celebrating queer pride and strength. We will also recognize the empowering role beauty might play in lesbians' lives. bell hooks (1995) notes that learning to recognize and see beauty "is an act of resistance in a culture of domination" (p. 124). Doing beauty, in this context, enables not only a multiplicity of looks, but also new ways of formulating and validating individual, couple, and community identities.

NOTE

1. Among the 50 women comprising the sample for the larger study, the average age was 28 years, with a range from 19 to 50 years. The women were asked to self-identify ethnicity: four were African American; eight were Latina/Mexican American; three were Asian American; one was South Asian; the remainder (68%)

were European American or Caucasian. Many of the respondents were students pursuing graduate or undergraduate degrees (70%); those in the professional sphere worked in the service industries, office administration, research, management, and counseling. Two women were unemployed.

REFERENCES

de Beauvoir, S. (1952). *The second sex* (H.M. Parshley, trans). New York: Vintage Books.

Chapkis, W. (1986). *Beauty secrets: Women and the politics of appearance.* Boston, MA: South End Press.

Evans, C., and Thorton, M. (1989). *Women & Fashion: A new look.* London: Quartet Books.

Everett, K. & Christopher, P. (1992). *Framing lesbian fashion* (film). San Francisco: Frameline and London: Cinenova (distributors).

Freitas, A., Kaiser, S.B., and Hammidi, T. (1996). Communities, commodities, cultural space, and style. *Journal of Homosexuality, 31*(1/2), 83-107.

hooks, b. (1995). *Art on my mind: Visual politics.* New York, NY: New Press.

MacCannell, D., and MacCannell, J.F. (1987). The beauty system. In N. Armstrong and L. Tennenhouse (eds.). *The ideology of conduct: Essays on literature and the history of sexuality.* New York: Methuen.

MacCannell, D., & MacCannell, J.F. (1987). The beauty system. In N. Armstrong and L. Tennehouse (eds.). *The ideology of conduct: Essays on literature and the history of sexuality* (pp. 206-238). New York: Methuen.

Olesen, V. (1994). Feminisms and models of qualitative research. In N.K. Denzin and Y.S. Lincoln (eds.). *Handbook of qualitative research* (pp. 158-174). Thousand Oaks, CA: Sage Publications.

Tseelon, E. (1995). *The masque of femininity.* London: Sage Publications.

Wolf, N. (1991). *The beauty myth: How images of beauty are used against women.* New York, NY: William Morrow and Company, Inc.

Listen to the Roars and Whispers of Water

Jeanine C. Cogan

The cool mountain waterfall pours
down from the sky over my undressed
body offering her wisdom for
how to live beautifully.

"Allow emotions to rush through you
with such vigor you become giddy like an
eleven month old baby discovering
her feet will take her places still
unknown. Or a teenager
on a roller coaster ride feeling
her stomach rise and fall with the rise
and fall down an endless
drop into danger. Or a sweat drenched
woman tasting her own
salt soaked skin in the delirious afterglow
of her first orgasm."

"Pour your life giving spirit onto others
generously. Rejuvenate and massage the
tired and lifeless
until they rediscover
their indigenous selves."

This poem inspired by Maui experiences, 1999.

[Haworth co-indexing entry note]: "Listen to the Roars and Whispers of Water." Cogan, Jeanine C. Co-published simultaneously in *Journal of Lesbian Studies* (The Haworth Press, Inc.) Vol. 3, No. 4, 1999, pp. 65-66; and: *Lesbians, Levis and Lipstick: The Meaning of Beauty in Our Lives* (ed: Jeanine C. Cogan and Joanie M. Erickson) The Haworth Press, Inc., 1999, pp. 65-66; and: *Lesbians, Levis and Lipstick: The Meaning of Beauty in Our Lives* (ed: Jeanine C. Cogan and Joanie M. Erickson) Harrington Park Press, an imprint of The Haworth Press, Inc., 1999, pp. 65-66. Single or multiple copies of this article are available for a fee from The Haworth Document Delivery Service [1-800-342-9678, 9:00 a.m. - 5:00 p.m. (EST). E-mail address: getinfo@haworthpressinc.com].

And the still ocean whispers,
"Take time to appreciate the earth's
tranquility and make friends with your
peaceful soul.
Experience the gentle kiss of the wind
against your bare breasts."

"Admire the ginger flowers. Taste an
overripe mango just picked and enjoy the
sweet stickiness as its juice slips
delicately down your chin.
Take a moment to walk with the white
wild cat who has adventures to teach.
Read a good book lazily among the
plentiful Taro leaves.
Pick your guiding star from the balsamic
sky. Make a wish upon the pastel
rainbow that greets you in the early
morning drizzle."

"And remember *you* are the earth, moon,
sun, fire, water, and sky.
The stars you reach for exist inside, the
expansive sky you long to touch is there
within you–buried underneath the
layers of chaos. Peel back those layers
and you will find the mountain waterfalls,
the still ocean. Drink the water, you drink
in yourself. Heal the earth, you heal.
With each new moon and gracious
sunrise let go, begin anew, and live
beautifully."

PART II

FREEDOMS
AND CONSTRAINTS
OF LESBIAN BEAUTY NORMS

Lesbian beauty is a message, means of communication,
a release, less tied to the beauty of dominant culture;
the 36-24-36 Barbie ideal.

Lesbian beauty is more of a freedom and ease, but sometimes also
of a rigidity, less crossable lines, beauty and
fashion are intermingled and locked into particular roles.

Confessions of a Butch Straight Woman

Joanie M. Erickson

SUMMARY. According to stereotypical homosexual images of the stone-faced woman stomping around in work boots, lesbians adopt a more masculine demeanor and style of dress after coming out. In this article the author debunks this notion by sharing her personal experience of how her appearance changed through the course of her coming out process. She contrasts her views about beauty and how she felt about her body when she lived as a straight woman to her newfound comfort and freedom as a lesbian expressing the feminine and masculine sides of herself. In an ironic twist, coming out allowed her to shed the heterosexual beauty prescriptions, reconnect with her feminine side, and come out as beautiful. *[Article copies available for a fee from The Haworth Document Delivery Service: 1-800-342-9678. E-mail address: getinfo@ haworthpressinc.com]*

I spent the first 10 years of my adult life trapped inside the body of a straight woman. That heterosexual body of mine married, had a child and walked around as if attracting male attention was the Olympic gold medal of womanhood. But beneath the flesh that slept beside men, frolicked with them in the back seat of cars, and touched them while dancing, beat the heart of a

---

Joanie M. Erickson is a public relations director for a non-profit healthcare organization. She has also worked as a newspaper reporter and a copywriter. She lives in Davis, California, with her daughter and a pack of cats.

Address correspondence to: Joanie M. Erickson, 3215 Bermuda Avenue, #10, Davis, CA 95616 (E-mail: Jrytes@aol.com).

Author Note: Joanie thanks Jeanine Cogan for the opportunity to write this article, her friendship, and all those really great earrings.

[Haworth co-indexing entry note]: "Confessions of a Butch Straight Woman." Erickson, Joanie M. Co-published simultaneously in *Journal of Lesbian Studies* (The Haworth Press, Inc.) Vol. 3, No. 4, 1999, pp. 69-72; and: *Lesbians, Levis and Lipstick: The Meaning of Beauty in Our Lives* (ed: Jeanine C. Cogan and Joanie M. Erickson) The Haworth Press, Inc., 1999, pp. 69-72; and: *Lesbians, Levis and Lipstick: The Meaning of Beauty in Our Lives* (ed: Jeanine C. Cogan and Joanie M. Erickson) Harrington Park Press, an imprint of The Haworth Press, Inc., 1999, pp. 69-72. Single or multiple copies of this article are available for a fee from The Haworth Document Delivery Service [1-800-342-9678, 9:00 a.m. - 5:00 p.m. (EST). E-mail address: getinfo@haworthpressinc.com].

69

lesbian. I can't remember a time when I wasn't crushed out on some neighbor girl, her mother, or a teacher with soft skin and a kind voice. I still consider my fifth grade teacher, Ms. Basil, to be the love of my life.

Alas, too much religion and social pressure kept me on the straight and narrow path. I tried so hard to be a good heterosexual, I swear I did, but I failed. Fortunately, by the age of 30 I found the courage to be the lesbian that I was. In a very short time, I said good bye to the husband, the suburban tract home and most of my Tupperware. Of course, I did keep my daughter, Anna, who is an incredibly wonderful human being and having her is one of the best decisions I ever made. She could be a poster child for serial bi-sexuality in the childbearing years; I know artificial insemination works, too, but with a father around, I get an occasional weekend off.

As I became more comfortable in my lesbian skin and evolved from describing myself first as bisexual, then as gay (in a very quiet voice) to calling myself a lesbian as comfortably as I call myself blonde, I tempered a part of myself that, for me, was strangely associated with my life as a heterosexual: my butchness. Yes, I was a butch straight woman. I wore flannel; I wore men's clothes; I swayed my shoulders when I walked (never my hips). I walked about protected by an armor of masculinity.

I was the classic tomboy as a child, a memory many lesbians share. My favorite playmates were my older brother and his friends. I preferred boys' jeans to girls', t-shirts to blouses and liked my hair cut short. While the other girls in the neighborhood played with Barbie, I could usually be found up a tree or collecting bugs. In fantasy play with other children I would only participate if I could be a boy. Boys had adventures: they went to work and fought fires and captured criminals; they were doctors, soldiers and baseball players. As far as I could tell, girls did little more than wait for the men: they mopped the floors; they cooked the meals; they rocked the babies; and if they were really lucky they got to tend to the wounded.

Early on I realized that in my world masculinity was equated with power and femininity with submission. Every ruffle on my shirt or ribbon in my hair meant giving up control of my destiny. Of course, feminine beauty had its power, as well. I was not oblivious to the fact that the boys who wanted to play football with me in the street or wanted to study with me didn't make me valentines, or later, ask me to dances. The girls with long hair and delicate limbs caused men of all ages to orbit about them with a powerful pull. But I knew that this form of female power–beauty–was impossible for me to attain because I possessed the fatal flaw: fat.

By the time I reached adolescence, I went from being a gangly, sure-footed girl, to a round, tall adolescent. The teenager in the mirror looked more like my large Swedish aunts every day. By junior high I was 5′8″ and wore a size 14. At my junior high locker and in the PE dressing room I learned that fat and beautiful were oxymorons in my culture. I came to believe I didn't have the capacity, or permission, to be beautiful. I couldn't wield power with a short skirt or Farrah Fawcett hair. My attempts at beauty seemed to bring only ridicule or the kind of male attention that made me feel dirty and demeaned, not admired or respected. So, as a teen and young woman I rarely tried to be beautiful. When I did "dress up"–do my hair, wear make-up, or attempt any other conventional beauty rituals–I felt like I was dressed up for a costume party or living in someone else's body, a straight woman's body. I felt exposed and vulnerable until I shed the dress, jumped in the shower to return my hair and face to its natural state, and slipped on a pair of jeans.

After I graduated from college and began a career, I learned to dress like a generic professional woman, a mere imitation of the women I worked with who had classic feminine styling and knew how to tie scarves. I look at pictures of me as a young professional and laugh. One of my favorites is of me in lipstick, rouge and this red "power dress" with ruffles, teetering about on high-heeled, pointed-toe pumps. I was dressed exactly how I thought I should dress to be accepted, even though I looked like a guy in drag. Well, I guess I shouldn't insult my cross-dressing brothers. They looked better than I did because they know how to accessorize; they know how to make themselves pretty. I only knew how to put on the work uniform and hope for the best.

When I came out as a lesbian, I came out as a beautiful woman. Although the lesbian culture isn't immune from fat oppression, tall, large Nordic-looking women are often considered attractive. Furthermore, my humor, intelligence and gentleness seemed to be as important to most of my potential partners as my waistline. About six months after coming out, a lesbian friend actually referred to me as "a catch." Me, a 5'9" 200 lb. catch! Suddenly, I saw myself as potentially beautiful.

Today, I enjoy the less constraining lesbian beauty norms that allow me to explore both the feminine and masculine sides of myself. Sometimes I wake up on what I call "the butch side of the bed." On those days I prefer tailored cotton shirts and jackets at work, and sweats or flannel on the weekends. I take larger steps; I walk with my knuckles pointing away from my body instead of swaying at my sides. I feel larger, more charismatic and I want the whole world to know that I'm a dyke with a better-looking partner than any man in the room has.

On my femme days I flirt with my newfound love: accessories. As a straight woman, I never cared if my belt matched my shoes. Now, the belt, the shoes and the purse (yes, even a purse) simply must match. The earrings and necklace (which also match) should bring out complimentary colors in my outfit. And Joanie the Big Beautiful Lesbian can tie a silk scarf in less than 10 seconds. When I'm feeling femme, the sway that used to reside in my shoulders when I walked moves farther south with every step. By the time I'm 40, I'm sure that sway will make it all the way to my hips.

I've also quit dressing in the costume that I think is appropriate for women in a business or social setting. I now have my own style that makes me feel good about the way I look. I've abandoned the "man in a red dress" look for slacks, jackets and silk shirts. I rarely wear a dress anymore, but I feel softer and more feminine than in any other period of my life. Yet, this kind of femininity doesn't rob me of a thing. I am also more competent and respected than in any time of my life. Being with women has softened me and beauty doesn't scare me anymore.

When working on this publication, my nine-year-old daughter Anna begged to be quoted. Jeanine, my co-editor, and I told her she had to contribute a new thought or idea to be included. So she began thinking about lesbians and beauty, searching deep in her 4th grade psyche for profound thoughts. She came up with a definition of lesbian beauty that, for me, typifies my experience as coming out as a lesbian and a beautiful woman.

"I don't think there's any difference between straight women and lesbians," she said after a full minute of contemplation. "Some straight women aren't that pretty, and some lesbians aren't that pretty. Some straight women are pretty, and some lesbians are pretty. There's no difference . . . except for lesbians laugh more, and I guess that makes them prettier." My daughter is a genius.

Invisible Woman

Beth Daily-Wallach

I am the woman that no woman sees.
I don't fit the image we have of a dyke.
Ballet and life have taught me to strive
to camouflage strength beneath gliding grace.
No one should see muscles moving my weight,
nor feel the Will that frees me to fly.

But I save my glances for the dyke.

Men strut by with arrogant assuming,
in work shirts and jeans, or suit coats and ties.
They know that they have the world's full attention,
that their glance makes or breaks a lady's day.
Tripping over me in awe when I don't step aside,
they search my eyes fiercely for reverence.

But I save my glances for the dyke.

Beth Daily-Wallach is a psychologist in private practice near Pittsburgh, and an amateur ballet dancer. She holds a master's degree in psychology from Edinboro University of Pennsylvania. She initially gave up femininity as her entrance fee into the lesbian feminist community, and is now learning to integrate her feminist and feminine identities with the loving support of her life partner, an old-fashioned butch.

Address correspondence to: Beth Daily-Wallach, 2809 Old Washington Road, Bridgeville, PA 15017.

[Haworth co-indexing entry note]: "Invisible Woman." Daily-Wallach, Beth. Co-published simultaneously in *Journal of Lesbian Studies* (The Haworth Press, Inc.) Vol. 3, No. 4, 1999, pp. 73-75; and: *Lesbians, Levis and Lipstick: The Meaning of Beauty in Our Lives* (ed: Jeanine C. Cogan and Joanie M. Erickson) The Haworth Press, Inc., 1999, pp. 73-75; and: *Lesbians, Levis and Lipstick: The Meaning of Beauty in Our Lives* (ed: Jeanine C. Cogan and Joanie M. Erickson) Harrington Park Press, an imprint of The Haworth Press, Inc., 1999, pp. 73-75. Single or multiple copies of this article are available for a fee from The Haworth Document Delivery Service [1-800-342-9678, 9:00 a.m. - 5:00 p.m. (EST). E-mail address: getinfo@haworthpressinc.com].

I scan the sea of faces ahead,
searching for Her, for Us, for Me.
I long for her eyes, for her smile to meet mine,
to affirm me, to know me, to briefly connect,
in a world that rarely sees me for who I am.

As I save my glances for the dyke.

I spot her stride before her face.
Big or small, she takes up space.
She moves sure-footed in high-tops and jeans,
or glares out from above a tailored skirt and heels.
I lock my eyes on her strength, her courage,
as she defies roles with her butch existence.

I save my glances for the dyke

But will she see me? Will she know who I am?
Or will long blowing hair hide my flirting smile,
my earcuff, my proudly unpainted face?
Will ballet pink legs darting under a skirt
overshadow my sensible shoes and sure gait?

As she saves her glances for the dyke.

Does she know I share much of her life:
her dreams, her fears, lost families and pain?
Does she think invisibility shields me from hate?
Does she resent my inability to pass as a butch?

Does she know my glances are saved for the dyke?

Hey Womon, look at me! Please know who I am.
I am the lover you seek at the bars.
I am your beloved and despised mirror image:
the deepening of your curves and softening of your power,
the coaxing of tears you pretend not to cry,
your invisible pillar of comfort and strength.
My love can make you beautiful and whole,
as pink and slate blue meld proudly to lavender,
as curry with cinnamon lights fire on the tongue.

As you save your glances for the dyke.

She comes closer now–I catch my breath.
I seek her smile as the distance narrows.
Will she see herself reflected in my eyes?
Or will she pass by with practiced indifference,
looking beyond me as she searches up the street.
Looking for Herself, for Us, for Me.

As she saves her glances for the dyke.

How many times has she misread my stare,
blinded by an image she thinks we all fit?
How often have I, similarly blind,
walked lonely, indifferent, past the mirror I seek,
seeing someone else's reflection in her eyes.

As I save my glances for the dyke.

Lesbians Walk the Tightrope of Beauty: Thin Is In but Femme Is Out

Jeanine C. Cogan

SUMMARY. This research addressed how lesbians are influenced by and respond to beauty constructions of dominant culture while they simultaneously redefine and create their own meaning of beauty within lesbian communities. A sample of 181 lesbian and bisexual women from the Sacramento area completed a survey examining their reasons for exercising, amount and type of exercise, body image and satisfaction with weight, eating disorder symptoms, perceptions of lesbian health threats, degree of feminist identification, appearance as a form of lesbian identification, and change of appearance after coming out. Whereas feminism served as a buffer against negative body image, the body image results found lesbians to be bound to dominant culture's thinness expectations. Other findings, however, also suggest that lesbians define beauty in their own unique way. Moving beyond simply responding to traditional beauty pressures, lesbians in this study also used beauty markers as a creative strategy to find and identify each other, suggesting that one purpose of lesbian beauty is functional. *[Article copies available for a fee from The Haworth Document Delivery Service: 1-800-342-9678. E-mail address: getinfo@haworthpressinc.com]*

Jeanine C. Cogan, PhD, is a social psychologist conducting research on the social construction of beauty and the ramifications of not fitting into culturally prescribed norms. She worked in Washington, DC, as the James Marshall Public Policy Scholar, awarded by the Society for the Psychological Study of Social Issues, where she focused on federal policy addressing the lives and experiences of lesbian, gay, and bisexual individuals as well as other social issues.

[Haworth co-indexing entry note]: "Lesbians Walk the Tightrope of Beauty: Thin Is In but Femme Is Out." Cogan, Jeanine C. Co-published simultaneously in *Journal of Lesbian Studies* (The Haworth Press, Inc.) Vol. 3, No. 4, 1999, pp. 77-89; and: *Lesbians, Levis and Lipstick: The Meaning of Beauty in Our Lives* (ed: Jeanine C. Cogan and Joanie M. Erickson) The Haworth Press, Inc., 1999, pp. 77-89; and: *Lesbians, Levis and Lipstick: The Meaning of Beauty in Our Lives* (ed: Jeanine C. Cogan and Joanie M. Erickson) Harrington Park Press, an imprint of The Haworth Press, Inc., 1999, pp. 77-89. Single or multiple copies of this article are available for a fee from The Haworth Document Delivery Service [1-800-342-9678, 9:00 a.m. - 5:00 p.m. (EST). E-mail address: getinfo@haworthpressinc.com].

77

In a number of open forums I conducted on the topic of lesbian beauty, enthusiasm and ambivalence collided together to create a dynamic conversation where the contradicting themes of freedom and distress co-exist. Lesbians talked about the freedom they experience after coming out to abandon traditional beauty expectations that trapped them into heels, dresses and big hair–which for some felt clown-like and uncomfortable. As this woman summarized, "Lesbian beauty is a release. We are not tied to the beauty of dominant culture–the 36-24-36 Barbie ideal. There is more of a freedom and ease." Yet lesbians also shared their frustration with the unwritten rules of lesbian beauty where certain styles are considered manifestations of appropriate lesbian presentation while others are deemed unacceptable. As one woman expressed, "With my feminine appearance I get a strange dual reaction from other lesbians. Either a repulsion to my femininity, which they associate with weakness, or a hungry and judgmental objectification. Both are uncomfortable."

Why, after escaping oppressive traditional beauty norms, would lesbians, similarly, create confining norms within their own lesbian communities? To answer this question we must consider how lesbians are influenced by and respond to beauty constructions of dominant culture and how they simultaneously redefine and create their own meanings of beauty within lesbian communities. That was the purpose of this research study.

DESCRIPTION OF THE CURRENT STUDY

At a summer gay pride fair in Sacramento, California, 181 women ranging in age from 17 to 58 years, with a mean age of 34, completed an anonymous questionnaire. Eighty-eight percent of the women self-identified as lesbian and 12% as bisexual.[1] Education ranged from high school or less to having received a doctorate degree, with the mean education of an associate's degree or equivalent. The mean annual income was a range of $20,000-25,000, with a bimodal distribution of $5,000-15,000 and more than $40,000. Most women were employed (81%) and 25% were students. Almost three-quarters of the sample (n = 132, 73%) identified as white, 8% (n = 15) as Latina, 7% (n = 12) as Asian American, 6% (n = 11) as African American, 4% (n = 7) as Native American and 2% (n = 4) as mixed race. This racial composition reflects the demographics of the larger gay, lesbian, bisexual community in Sacramento.[2]

HOW LESBIANS ARE INFLUENCED
BY DOMINANT CULTURE'S BEAUTY CONSTRUCTIONS

Reasons for Exercise: Are We Striving to Attain the Barbie Mandate?

In a culture where beauty is the currency of success for women, exercise is often simply another strategy for weight control, becoming more physically attractive, and toned. Do lesbians also strive toward this Barbie mandate or do they exercise for non-aesthetic reasons? Heffernan (1996) found that lesbians were most likely to exercise for health and fitness reasons rather than to lose weight.

To further address this question, a 24-item scale[3] developed by Silberstein et al. (1989) was adapted. This scale examines the reasons why people exercise along seven different dimensions. For the purposes of this study these seven dimensions were further organized into two categories: (1) exercising for aesthetic reasons and (2) exercising for non-aesthetic reasons. Aesthetic reasons for exercising were: for weight control, physical attractiveness and to improve body tone. Non-aesthetic reasons for exercising were: for improving overall health, fitness, mood, and for enjoyment. Women rated how important each reason was in determining why they exercise on a 4-point rating scale (0 = not at all important, 3 = very important).

Did Women Exercise for Mainly Aesthetic Reasons? No, women in this sample were significantly more likely to exercise for non-aesthetic reasons (M = 1.9, SD = .61) than aesthetic reasons (M = 1.7, SD = .79) [t(169) = 4.6, p. = .00]. Only 9.4% of women were more likely to exercise for aesthetic reasons, that is to attract others (M = 1.68), for weight control (M = 1.64), and to tone their bodies (M = 1.67) than non-aesthetic reasons, that is to maintain health (M = 2.32), for fitness (M = 2.14), to improve mood (M = 2.01) and simply for the enjoyment (M = 1.21).

These findings indicate that lesbians and bisexual women in this sample exercised for more functional reasons rather than to attain traditional beauty goals. This finding is similar to research by Striegel-Moore and colleagues (1990) in which lesbians valued the ability of their bodies to be functional, and subsequently, well-functioning bodies were associated with higher self-esteem.

How Much and What Type of Fitness Activities Did Women Engage In?

Any athletic female is perceived as or accused of being a lesbian, giving birth to the stereotype that all softball players are lesbian and all lesbians are softball players. Other than such stereotypes, however, what do we really know about the amounts and types of physical activities lesbians enjoy? To answer this question the author designed a questionnaire where women indicated on a 6-point rating scale the number of hours spent (0 = 0 hours, 5 = 10+ hours) engaging in each of 15 possible activities over the past month (refer to Table 1).

On average lesbian and bisexual women in the sample engaged in four different activities in the past month. Contrary to the "all lesbians are softball players" stereotype, only 10% of the women in this sample played softball. Other activities such as walking, dancing, hiking and weight lifting were

TABLE 1. The Number of Women Participating, Percentage of Participation, and Mean Number of Hours Spent by Type of Activity

Type of Activity	Number participating in this activity	% participating in this activity	Mean number of hours per month
Walking	168	96%	4-5 hrs
Dancing	94	55%	4-5 hrs
Hiking/Camping	69	40%	4-5 hrs
Weight Lifting	67	39%	4-5 hrs
Biking	66	37%	4-5 hrs
Swimming	55	32%	2-3 hrs
Running	42	25%	2-3 hrs
Other	34	20%	6-10 hrs
Aerobics	29	17%	2-3 hrs
Basketball	19	11%	2-3 hrs
Softball	18	11%	4-5 hrs
Tennis/Racquetball	17	10%	2-3 hrs
Roller Blading	17	10%	2-3 hrs
Martial Arts	12	7%	4-5 hrs
Volleyball	9	5%	2-3 hrs

Note: Of those who specified what kind of *Other* activity they engaged in (n = 31) the most common response was sex (29%), followed by indoor exercise such as the Stairmaster or treadmill (19%) and golf (9%).

more popular among women in this sample. Walking was rated as the most frequent activity women engaged in (96%) and volleyball as the least frequent activity (5%).

How Do Lesbians Feel About Their Bodies?
The Influence of Thinness Expectations

A recurring question authors in this volume address is whether lesbians internalize and pursue dominant culture's thinness ideal (see Heffernan, this volume). The answer, though research is not conclusive, has basically been yes; to some extent, lesbians yearn for the Barbie image which manifests itself in similar rates of body dissatisfaction as heterosexual women. To make sense of the complex and at times contradicting findings it may be useful to distinguish the extreme forms of body dissatisfaction (eating disorder symptoms) from what has been called normative female discontent (e.g., feeling too fat). Body image was assessed accordingly among the women in this sample.

Weight, Ideal Weight and Dieting Behavior. Through weight and height data the Body Mass Index (BMI) was calculated. BMI is the most reliable and valid measure of weight, which accounts for height and is calculated by dividing weight by height squared. Additionally, individuals were asked what their ideal weight was, allowing for the calculation of the weight discrepancy score which was the difference between their *current* and *ideal* weights. A last question asked whether individuals were currently on a diet to lose weight.

Are Lesbians Satisfied with Their Weight? No, on average women wanted to be thinner than their current weight, with the mean weight of 167.9 lbs. (SD = 42.8; BMI: M = 24.5, SD = 6.2) which differed significantly from the mean *ideal* weight of 136.6 lbs. [t(166) = 10.6, p = .00]. The mean discrepancy score between *real* and *ideal* weight was 30.9 lbs. (SD = 39 lbs.), indicating that on average women wanted to weigh 31 lbs. *less* than their current weight. Only ten percent of women indicated no difference between their *real* and *ideal* weights, suggesting they were satisfied with their current weight. Of the 90% of women who were dissatisfied with their current weight 86% wanted to weigh *less* than their current weight and four percent (N = 7) wanted to weigh *more*.

Variables associated with greater dissatisfaction with current weight were age and BMI, with older and heavier women having higher weight discrepancy scores. Analyses revealed significant positive correlations between the weight discrepancy score and age (r = .17, p = .03) and BMI (r = .85, p = .000). Though weight dissatisfaction was high, the percentage of women who were dieting to lose weight was relatively low with 19% of the total sample of women currently dieting to lose weight.

Did Lesbians Display Eating Disorder Symptoms? To answer this question respondents completed three subscales of the 64-item Eating Disorder Inventory developed by Garner, Olmsted, and Polivy (1983): the Drive for Thinness, the Bulimia, and the Body Dissatisfaction subscales. Items were scored on 6-point rating scale (1 = never, 6 = always), where high scores corresponded to more negative body image. The mean score on the Bulimia subscale was 2.1 (SD = .92), indicating that women in this sample *rarely* manifested bulimic symptoms. However, it is also worthy to note that 10% of the sample said they currently engaged in bulimic symptoms (such as bingeing, thinking of vomiting to lose weight, and eating in secrecy) *sometimes* to *always*. The mean score on the Drive for Thinness subscale was 2.78 (SD = 1.15), indicating that women *sometimes* strived toward thinness (e.g., I think about dieting, I am preoccupied with the desire to be thinner). And the mean score on the Body Dissatisfaction subscale was a 3.97 (SD = 1.25), indicating that women were *often* dissatisfied with their bodies (e.g., I think my stomach is too big, hips are too big). When comparing these findings to a sample of U.S. heterosexual women (see Cogan, Bhalla, Sefa-Dedeh & Rothblum, 1996), the lesbians in this sample were less likely to manifest symptoms of Bulimia and Drive for Thinness yet were similarly often engaged in Body Dissatisfaction.[4]

Similar to Heffernan's findings (this volume), the more women deviated from how much they perceived they should ideally weigh (as measured by the weight discrepancy score) the more their body discontent. Weight discrepancy scores were positively correlated with all three subscales, indicating that a woman with a higher weight discrepancy scored higher on the bulimia subscale (r = .35, p = .00), the body dissatisfaction subscale (r = .54, p = .00), and the drive for thinness subscale (r = .29, p = .00).

Don't Ask, Don't Tell: The Hidden Discontent

These findings corroborate other research suggesting that lesbians do struggle with body image issues. Negative evaluations of their bodies (e.g., hips too big) and a desire to weigh less, characteristic of normative female discontent, were not uncommon. What is potentially dangerous for lesbians is a tension between the outside expectations within lesbian communities for size acceptance/body love and lesbians' internal experiences. As one woman wrote on the survey, "How can I know so much about women and body image and still have so much loathing for my own body?" The small number of women who were currently dieting or used exercise to lose weight in contrast to the high number who were dissatisfied with their weight may be a manifestation of this tension. As Striegel-Moore and her colleagues (1990) hypothesized, lesbians are less likely to diet because it is not socially sanctioned within their lesbian communities for it is seen as "buying into" dominant culture's definitions of beauty.[5]

Additional evidence for this potential tension can be found in the preliminary results of data I am currently analyzing with more than 700 lesbians. The women in this sample rated what would be considered the ideal figure for lesbians as significantly bigger than what they perceived to be ideal for women in general. Yet similar to the findings in this study, body dissatisfaction was common. If the expectation is that "lesbians should accept and love large bodies" yet their inner experience of their own bodies is quite the contrary, then there is little room for lesbians to seek support for negative body image, which thus remains hidden. The existence and prevalence of negative body image and eating disorder symptoms among lesbians need to be openly addressed within our communities.

Body Image as a Health Threat

Although body image is rarely constructed by dominant culture as in and of itself a health threat, body hatred is psychologically debilitating and most often serves as a precursor to the development of eating disorders (e.g., see

Cogan for review, 1999). Based on responses from women in a pilot study (unpublished) the author designed a measure examining lesbian health threats. Women were asked to rate on a 4-point rating scale (0 = not at all threatening, 3 = very threatening) how threatening they perceived each of 12 health issues (refer to Table 2) to be for lesbian and bisexual women.

Is Body Image Perceived as a Lesbian Health Threat? Yes, to some extent. Results showed that women rated body image issues/dissatisfaction with body as *fairly* threatening to lesbian health, therefore, suggesting a recognition of this as a lesbian health issue. Yet this is in the context of lesbians rating all other issues as *fairly* threatening except for discrimination based on sexual orientation, which was rated as very threatening. Body image issues were rated as 8th most threatening out of 12 issues; significantly *less* threatening than the highest rated health issue, discrimination based on sexual orientation [= 2.55, t(177) = 5.7, p. = .00] and significantly *more* threatening than the lowest rated health issues, AIDS and aging, both with means of 1.76 [t(174) = 4.0, p. = .00].

Since relatively little is currently known about health issues that threaten lesbian and bisexual women, we cannot judge whether this evaluation of body dissatisfaction as a health threat is an over, under or accurate estimate of the actual threat experienced and how this may compare to other health issues.

How to Escape the Chains of Negative Body Image: Are Bra Burners on the Right Track?

Given that negative body image is common among lesbians, how can positive body image be promoted? One answer that others have also hypothe-

TABLE 2. Means and Standard Deviations by Health Threat

Health Threat	Mean	Standard Deviation
Discrimination based on sexual orientation	2.55	.72
Violence against women	2.53	.75
Breast cancer	2.50	.84
Depression	2.39	.76
Alcohol or drug abuse	2.37	.81
Work-related stress	2.21	.86
Lack of, or no access to health care	2.18	.89
Body image issues/dissatisfaction with our bodies	2.13	.85
Other forms of cancer	2.05	.85
Gynecological problems	1.94	.84
Issues related to aging	1.76	.87
AIDS	1.76	.94

Notes: On a scale where 3 = very threatening, 2 = fairly threatening, 1 = somewhat threatening, 0 = not at all threatening.

sized, though with mixed findings, may be feminism (Dionne, Davis, Fox, & Gurevich, 1995; Guille & Chrisler, this volume; Heffernan, 1996). Inherent in a feminist philosophy is the value of women in all their diversity. The process of identifying as a feminist includes a critical analysis of societal institutions and practices that serve to disempower women and limit their social, economic and political freedoms. Many feminists challenge socialized female beauty mandates that serve to trap women into preoccupation with attaining the unattainable. Given this analysis, lesbians who identify with such feminist ideas likely have healthier body image.

Does Feminism Serve as a Buffer Against Negative Body Image?

Since researchers have pointed to measurement issues as one explanation for mixed findings on this topic, I employed two measures of feminism (1) the degree of feminist self-labeling and (2) attitudes toward the women's movement. Analyses on both measures indicated that *women who identified strongly with feminism were more likely to be satisfied with their bodies than those who did not.*

First Measure: The Degree of Feminist Self-Labeling. The question, "How much do you consider yourself a feminist?" asked women to self-label the degree to which they perceived themselves to be feminist (0 = not at all feminist, 9 = very much a feminist). The mean score was 6.2 (SD = 2.4), indicating that women self-identified as fairly feminist. The majority of women in this sample (72%) rated themselves as *somewhat* to *very* feminist (five or higher) with only three percent of women identifying themselves as *not at all* feminist (zero). The only demographic variable that was significantly correlated with the degree of feminist self-labeling was education (r = .23, p = .01), indicating that the more education women had the more they identified themselves as feminist.

Feminist self-labeling was recoded into a dichotomous variable of low and high feminist scores. Analysis of variance with feminist category as the independent variable and BMI and age as covariates (since they are significantly correlated with the body image measures) *indicated that high feminist scorers were more satisfied with their bodies than low feminist scorers.* Low feminist scorers had significantly higher means on the bulimia subscale [F(1,174) = 3.6, p = .02], the body dissatisfaction subscale [F(1,171) = 8.9, p = .01], the drive for thinness subscale [F(1,172) = 15.8, p = .00], and weight discrepancy scores [F(1,165) = 4.5, p = .05]. Low feminist scorers on average wanted to weigh 37.4 lbs. less than their current weight while high scorers wanted to weigh 29 lbs. less. Additionally, low feminist scorers were significantly more likely [F(1,169) = 12.1, p = .00] to exercise for aesthetic reasons (M = 1.93) than high scorers (M = 1.50)

Second Measure: Attitudes Toward Feminism and the Women's Movement.

This 10-item scale developed by Fassinger (1994) measured affective attitudes towards the women's movement on a 5-point rating scale (e.g., Feminist principles should be adopted everywhere; The women's movement has made important gains in equal rights and political power for women). Participants indicated their agreement with each statement (1 = strongly disagree, 5 = strongly agree).

The mean total score on endorsing the women's movement scale was a 41 (SD = 4.8), indicating high agreement with the values and goals of the women's movement (maximum possible score of 50). Scores on the attitudes toward the women's movement scale were recoded into a dichotomous variable distinguishing those who strongly endorsed and those who did not strongly endorse the women's movement. Analysis of variance with endorsement category as the independent variable and BMI and age as covariates *indicated that strong endorsers of the women's movement were more satisfied with their bodies than lower endorsers.* Lower endorsers of the women's movement had significantly higher means on the body dissatisfaction subscale [F(1,161) = 11.8, p = .001], the drive for thinness subscale [F(1,163) = 10.5, p = .00], and weight discrepancy scores [F(1,153) = 7.1, p = .01]. Lower endorsers on average wanted to weigh 32.4 lbs. less than their current weight while strong endorsers wanted to weigh 25 lbs. less than their current weight. Additionally, lower endorsers were significantly more likely [F(1,162) = 12.5, p = .00] to exercise for aesthetic reasons (M = 1.79) than strong endorsers (M = 1.32).

Contrary to other findings, for the lesbians in this sample both identifying as a feminist and endorsing the women's movement had a healthy influence on body image. This suggests that feminism may be a useful tool for unlearning internalized negative body image.

CREATING OUR OWN MEANINGS
OF BEAUTY WITHIN LESBIAN COMMUNITIES

Beauty Norms as Functional: Why Do Lesbians Wear Comfortable Shoes?

Given that lesbians have no easily identifiable attribute that allows us to recognize one another, creating our own codes of recognition is imperative. As a form of safety, to establish an identity, and to feel a sense of community, lesbians establish outward "I am a lesbian" markers. From the pinkie rings, to the Doc Martins, triangle earrings and certain haircuts, lesbian beauty norms, if we abide by them, help us find each other.

In her review article on lesbians and physical appearance Esther Rothblum (1994) theorized that lesbian beauty norms serve two specific functions: (1) to allow us to identify each other, and (2) to feel a sense of belonging to the group. To empirically examine the degree to which women create their appearance to be identified by other lesbians or to establish a sense of belonging to the group, the author designed the 5-item *Appearance as Lesbian Identification Scale*.[6] Women rated on a 4-point rating scale how true each statement was for them (0 = not at all true, 3 = very true).

Did Women Adopt an Appearance to Identify with Other Lesbians and Bisexuals? Yes, results showed that women in this sample *somewhat* agreed (Mean = .88) that their appearance was influenced by a desire to be identified as lesbians and feel a sense of belonging within the lesbian/bisexual community. Almost two-thirds of the sample (64%) endorsed the question "I dress in such a way that I may be identified as a lesbian by other lesbians" as true for them. More than half of the sample (56%) endorsed the question "I wear certain jewelry, buttons, or pins so that I may be identified as a lesbian by other lesbians" as true for them. More than half of the sample (54%) endorsed the question "I dress in such a way that I can feel a sense of belongingness within the lesbian community" as true for them.

Women were more likely to dress or have a haircut to be *identified* as lesbian/bisexual (M = 1.0) than to *feel a sense of belongingness* to the group (M = .70) [t(179) = 5.1, p = .00]. In terms of what markers women used to be identified as lesbian, they were more likely to adopt a certain *dress* (M = .94) than a specific *haircut* (M = .79) [t(177) = 3.6, p = .00].

These results lend empirical evidence to Rothblum's (1994) theory that lesbians use beauty to provide visible markers for identifying one another. These findings also offer a plausible answer to the question stated earlier, "Why, after escaping oppressive traditional beauty norms, would lesbians similarly create confining norms within their own lesbian communities?" Confining beauty norms may be an unintentional outcome of lesbians using beauty as an important function within lesbian culture. Establishing identifiable markers for recognizing one another is a creative solution to invisibility. The irony, however, is that lesbians who do not use these beauty markers are invisible.

How Did Appearance Change After Coming Out?

An avenue for examining the unique expressions of lesbian beauty is to address how their presentation changed after coming out. Respondents were asked whether their dress, style or appearance changed since they came out as lesbian or bisexual and more than a third of women (36%) said yes. Of those women, 45 offered an open-ended response to how their dress, style, or appearance had changed. Responses were grouped into eight categories (refer to Table 3).

Similar to the findings by Myers and her colleagues (this volume) and Hammidi and Kaiser (this volume), a common thread among many of these responses is the sense of freedom women felt from the constraining beauty expectations of dominant culture after coming out (i.e., comfortable dress,

TABLE 3. Open-Ended Responses for How Appearance Changed After Coming Out

Appearance Change	n	%
Cut hair	16	36%
Comfortable dress	10	22%
Gave up traditional beauty rituals (e.g., shaving, wearing make-up, dresses and high heels)	9	20%
Wore something to make self identifiable (e.g., jewelry, pins, boots)	7	16%
Got a tattoo or piercing	5	11%
Went from dressing for others to dressing for self	4	9%
More femme	4	9%
More butch	3	7%

gave up traditional beauty rituals, went from dressing for others to dressing for self). This feeling is well illustrated by the following woman's response, "I went from dressing how everybody thought girls should dress, to what I wanted to wear." A second common thread which further supports the finding that lesbians use expressions of beauty as a way to identify each other, is how women changed their appearance in order to be a noticeable member of the "lesbian club," so to speak (i.e., cut hair, wore something to make self identifiable, more butch [in some cases]). As one woman commented, "I wear a gold labyrinth necklace at all times and purposely make it visible to be out to others."

CONCLUSION

Though the body image results suggest that lesbians are partially bound to dominant culture's thinness expectations, other findings also suggest that lesbians assign their own meanings to beauty. Moving beyond simply responding to traditional beauty pressures, lesbians in this study used beauty markers as a creative strategy to find and identify each other. Within this context then, one purpose of lesbian beauty is clearly functional. A potential side effect to this functional purpose of beauty, however, is the invisibility of those lesbians who do not conform to expected lesbian looks. Given the frustration about the confining nature of lesbian beauty norms as discussed by many authors of this volume, the question remains, "How do we honor individual styles and expressions yet maintain the functional role beauty markers serve?" Further research addressing such questions will lead to a better understanding of this multi-dimensional topic.

NOTES

1. Sexual orientation was used as an independent variable in appropriate analyses and no differences based on sexual orientation resulted. The findings for lesbian and bisexual women are therefore discussed together.

2. The total sample size was not large enough for meaningful data analyses by race. Some trends seemed apparent yet due to the small numbers in each group there were no statistically significant differences. Unless otherwise stated, there were no differences on the measures and the demographic characteristics of sexual orientation, age, or socio-economic status.

3. All of the measures in this study had acceptable internal reliability, with Cronbach alphas of .75 or higher.

4. This comparison is not ideal due to the difference in mean age between the samples. Also, the actual means are not directly comparable due to different calculations of the scales. Therefore the reader must refer to the corresponding construct, e.g., in heterosexual study the mean of 1.42 indicates *often*, while in this study 3.97 indicates *often*.

5. Alternatively, however (though untested), a low rate of dieting among lesbians may reflect more knowledge about the ineffectiveness of restrictive dieting as a successful strategy for long-term weight loss.

6. The five items are: I dress in a way that I may be identified as a lesbian by other lesbians; I have a certain hair cut so that I may be identified as a lesbian by other lesbians; I wear certain jewelry, buttons, or pins so that I may be identified as a lesbian by other lesbians; I dress in such a way that I can feel a sense of belongingness within the lesbian community; I have a certain hair cut that allows me to feel a sense of connection with other lesbians (Cronbach alpha of scale = .85).

REFERENCES

Cogan, J.C. The social construction of obesity and eating disorders as pathological: Time for a paradigm shift. In J. Sobal and D. Maurer (Eds). *Interpreting Weight: The Social Management of Fatness and Thinness* (1999).

Cogan, J.C., Bhalla, S.K., Sefa-Dedeh, A., & Rothblum, E.D. (1996). A comparison study of United States and African students on perceptions of obesity and thinness. *Journal of Cross-Cultural Psychology, 27*, 98-113.

Dionne, M., Davis, C., Fox, J. & Gurevich, M. (1995). Feminist ideology as a predictor of body dissatisfaction in women. *Sex Roles, 33(3-4)* 277-287.

Fassinger, R.E. (1994). Development and testing of the attitudes toward feminism and the women's movement scale. *Psychology of Women Quarterly, 18*, 389-402.

Garner, D.M., Olmstead, M.P. & Polivy, J. (1983). Development and validation of a multidimensional eating disorders inventory for anorexia nervosa and bulimia. *International Journal of Eating Disorders, 2*, 15-34.

Heffernan, K. (1996). Eating disorders and weight concern among lesbians. *International Journal of Eating Disorders, 19*, 127-138.

Leavy, R. L. & Adams, E. M. (1986). Feminism as a correlate of self-esteem, self-acceptance, and social support among lesbians. *Psychology of Women Quarterly, 10*(4), 321-326.

Rothblum, E.D. (1994). Lesbians and physical appearance: Which model applies? In B. Greene and G.M. Herek (eds). *Psychological Perspectives on Lesbian and Gay Issues*. Thousand Oaks: Sage Publications.

Silberstein, L.R., Mishkind, M.E., Striegel-Moore, R.H., Timko, C. & Rodin, J. (1989). Men and their bodies: A comparison of homosexual and heterosexual men. *Psychosomatic Medicine, 51*, 337-346.

Striegel-Moore, R.H., Tucker, N., & Hsu, J. (1990). Body image dissatisfaction and disordered eating in lesbian college students. *International Journal of Eating Disorders, 9*, 493-500.

The Myth of the Short-Haired Lesbian

Dvora Zipkin

SUMMARY. A number of myths and misperceptions related to images of lesbian beauty surround hair length. Short hair has become a symbol of being a lesbian, and many lesbians with long hair have felt pressured to cut theirs when they come out. For this essay, seven white lesbians were interviewed regarding their long hair. They describe how, in choosing not to cut their hair, or to grow it long again, they are not recognized or taken seriously as lesbians, both by other lesbians and by heterosexuals. They feel that they are perceived as heterosexual or bisexual, questioning, just coming out, trying to pass as straight, or buying into male-defined standards of female beauty. This is in part because many lesbians have rejected traditionally "feminine" images of beauty, including long hair, and have placed a higher value on more "masculine" attributes, including short hair. In doing so, however, lesbians are still reacting to male-defined images and standards, and may be internalizing and perpetuating sexism. As more and more different kinds of women are coming out as lesbian, it becomes necessary to avoid making assumptions based on a woman's hair length. The time has come to create new images of who and what lesbians are and can be, and new standards of lesbian beauty. *[Article copies available for a fee from The Haworth Document Delivery Service: 1-800-342-9678. E-mail address: getinfo@haworthpressinc.com]*

Dvora Zipkin received her EdD from the School of Education at the University of Massachusetts Amherst in 1996, where she studied Human Development/Creativity and Diversity/Social Justice Education. Her dissertation, which explored the development of students' creative self-concept and the connections between creativity and social and personal change, was awarded second place in the first annual Odyssey of the Mind Dissertation Awards. Her most recent publication was in *Early Embraces: True-Life Stories of Women Describing Their First Lesbian Experience*, edited by Lindsey Elder (Alyson Publications, Los Angeles, 1996).

Address correspondence to: Dvora Zipkin, P.O. Box 1461, Greenfield, MA 01302.

[Haworth co-indexing entry note]: "The Myth of the Short-Haired Lesbian." Zipkin, Dvora. Co-published simultaneously in *Journal of Lesbian Studies* (The Haworth Press, Inc.) Vol. 3, No. 4, 1999, pp. 91-101; and: *Lesbians, Levis and Lipstick: The Meaning of Beauty in Our Lives* (ed: Jeanine C. Cogan and Joanie M. Erickson) The Haworth Press, Inc., 1999, pp. 91-101; and: *Lesbians, Levis and Lipstick: The Meaning of Beauty in Our Lives* (ed: Jeanine C. Cogan and Joanie M. Erickson) Harrington Park Press, an imprint of The Haworth Press, Inc., 1999, pp. 91-101. Single or multiple copies of this article are available for a fee from The Haworth Document Delivery Service [1-800-342-9678, 9:00 a.m. - 5:00 p.m. (EST). E-mail address: getinfo@haworthpressinc.com].

91

LONG-HAIRED LESBIANS;
OR, NOT ALL LONG-HAIRED WOMEN ARE STRAIGHT

I am a long-haired lesbian. I have had long hair since I was in high school in the 1960s, and when I came out in the early 1980s (in my early 30s), I saw no reason to cut it. My hair was a part of me and my self-image, and I liked the way it looked and felt. It became more of an issue a number of years later when I moved near Northampton ("Lesbianville, USA"), in western Massachusetts. As a single woman, I noticed that, unless at a lesbian event, I was not recognized as a lesbian. Walking the streets of Northampton, my inner "gaydar" would routinely go off when I saw other lesbians, but theirs never sounded when I passed by. Even at lesbian events, I was often the only woman present with hair below my ears (and mine comes well down my back), and more than once have felt suspected of not being a "real" lesbian.

Over two years, I had an on-going conversation with a long-haired friend, Maureen, with similar experiences. We decided to take a photograph of a group of lesbians with long hair to submit for the cover of the local Lesbian Calendar. The idea apparently struck a chord with a number of women: through word of mouth alone, we spoke to more than 20 long-haired lesbians, 14 of whom showed up one August evening in 1996 to take the photos. The month the picture appeared, we advertised a "long-haired lesbian potluck," and more than 20 new women showed up. These monthly potlucks have continued now for over a year (attracting both long- and short-haired women). We have found common ground in our frustrations and experiences of feeling unrecognized and dismissed as lesbians, misperceived as hetero-sexual (or as bisexual, but that's another story), and even judged by other lesbians because we kept our hair long. In fact, some local lesbians who saw our photo said that we kept our hair long because we were "trying to pass as straight," an interesting response since that photo on the front of the Lesbian Calendar would be displayed in bookstores all around the surrounding towns.

Based on my own experiences as a long-haired lesbian, I decided to interview seven women to further explore their experiences. Six of these women have long hair, while the seventh had long hair and cut it when she came out. Some of these women had been in the photo and some had not. All the women are white, two are Jewish, five live in western Massachusetts, one lives in Madison, Wisconsin, and one in Columbus, Ohio. They are between the ages of 28 and 47; five of the women identify as lesbian, while two are lesbian-identified bisexuals. They have been out anywhere between five years and "all of my life."

I asked each woman to tell me the history of her hair and why she chooses to keep it long, if she cut it or thought about cutting it when she first came out, and why or why not. I then asked them to talk about their experiences as lesbians with long hair: how they felt perceived by other lesbians and by heterosexuals and, if they had both experiences, how they felt perceived and treated differently with long hair and with short hair. Finally, I asked them for their own theories and explanations for the ways they've been perceived on the basis of their hair. Their stories illustrate a number of common experiences concerning invisibility and the fact that short-haired lesbians seem to be more easily recognizable and taken more seriously as lesbians.

COMING OUT PRESSURES: TO CUT OR NOT TO CUT?

Many lesbians feel some pressure to cut their hair when they come out. For some this comes from external expectations that that's the way lesbians "look," or from a desire to be recognized and to fit in; for others it's an internal process of wanting to make an outward change to reflect the inner changes in identity. Lisa thought about cutting her hair because she wanted to fit in: "I don't feel like a lot of [lesbians] take me very seriously when they see me, because they probably think I'm just experimenting: 'She's just following a whim, she's not really a lesbian.' " Susan, who has since grown her hair long again, cut hers when she came out because she was frustrated that no one recognized her as a lesbian, and because she wanted to be attractive to lesbians, not to men: "There's a different kind of beauty that's lesbian beauty . . . I wanted to be recognized in a sea of people and have some lesbian go, she's one of us, hey, how you doing?"

Chris, whose hair is still short, cut hers for both internal and external reasons:

> I think it was a way that I was getting in touch with my sexuality. It had to do with my image that lesbians were women with short hair . . . I really didn't see lesbians with long hair. . . . And I really do feel like to fit in, I needed to cut my hair short. I really did feel that way.

Taica and Kippy never thought about cutting their hair, in large part because they did not want to adjust themselves to the "norm." As Taica explained it, "Wanting long hair has been too much of an obsession with me my whole life to ever think I would cut my hair to fit in!"

The pressure still persists for many lesbians. When asked about the pressure to cut her hair, Maureen, who's been out for nearly ten years, responded, "Well, I feel like it now. I feel like if I had short hair, I'd be recognized more. . . . I have absolutely, positively felt that the best reason for having short hair would be that then I would be recognized as queer."

Long-haired lesbians say that they choose to keep their hair long for a number of reasons. For most of them, they simply love it that way; it is an integral part of their self-concept, and they could not imagine themselves with short hair. It feels good, it's beautiful and sensual, and it's practical. And another reason is resistance, as Emily voiced and other women echoed:

> Part of it is this resistance, to any assumptions that anyone wants to make about me. I don't like the idea that when you come out as a lesbian you're supposed to cut all your hair off and that's it. So it's a little of my contrary sort of nature, oh, is that what I'm supposed to do? Uh, huh, I don't think so.

OTHER LESBIANS' PERCEPTIONS OF LONG-HAIRED LESBIANS

The issues of recognition and acceptance are key ones for lesbians with long hair. Many feel like they are invisible as lesbians to other lesbians, or are not taken seriously. They feel like they are perceived as heterosexual, bisexual, questioning, or just coming out. As Lisa stated, "I think that when other lesbians first see me, they probably think that it's my first experience, that I probably haven't been out very long . . . I don't think they believe that I'm a lesbian." Taica also described how she is usually not perceived as a lesbian by other lesbians:

> When I'm with a short-haired lesbian, I'll see how my short-haired friend will get recognized and kind of get the eye, yeah, we recognize each other, we're both dykes, that little exchange of support. And it doesn't happen to me at all when I'm alone, not at all. If I try to give the look to another lesbian, she usually looks at me like, why is this straight woman staring at me?

Sometimes this non-recognition translates into feeling slighted, as Susan explained:

> When I was first coming out, I was invited to a Jewish lesbian Chanukah party, and I didn't know this at the time but there was a big controversy going on about whether or not non-lesbians should be invited. This one woman was so cold to me, and it turns out that she just assumed I was straight, and she was pissed off that I was there. And I was so annoyed by that, and I'm sure it's because how I looked–I don't look like a dyke.

In this regard, Emily compared her own experiences as both a short-haired straight woman and as a long-haired lesbian:

> I've had a lot of people make assumptions about me being straight or bisexual because of my hair. I sometimes feel lesbians making judg-

ments about me as sort of closeted: because I have long hair, I can pass. Because I can pass, I must be closeted. Because I must be closeted, I must be apolitical, I'm not contributing to the struggle. . . . I had the feeling that I didn't stand out as much in the lesbian community when I had short hair, that people accepted me more. Also, when I was straight and especially when I had short hair, a lot of people assumed I was a lesbian. I talked a lot about gay rights, and so I had people make that assumption, whereas now I talk about gay rights and people seem to assume very often that I'm a [heterosexual] ally. . . . I don't want the mainstream culture telling me how to look, and I don't want the alternative culture telling me how to look either.

Besides not being recognized as a lesbian in the wider lesbian community, women have had misassumptions made about them by friends and lovers. Susan illustrated this when she described her first meeting at a party with her now ex-girlfriend: "She didn't give me the time of day. Then we had a blind date. I recognized her and I said I met you at this party, and she said, I barely remember that, but I think I thought you were straight."

The first woman that Emily dated was uneasy with Emily's long hair:

[She] had a real issue with me growing my hair long . . . she would get her hair cut every month, and she would start to say to me, aren't you gonna get your hair cut? You know, your hair's getting kind of long, when are you going to cut your hair? She'd get really antsy. And I asked her, why does this bother you? Are you afraid what people are gonna think of me? And she said no, I'm afraid of what people are gonna think of me for seeing someone with long hair.

In spite of their personal experiences with not being recognized as lesbians, many long-haired lesbians do the same thing themselves. As Taica said, "I'm guilty of it myself to a degree; I'm sure there's lots of long-haired lesbians that I don't recognize as lesbians." And as Maureen put it, "That's how *I* recognize other lesbians! Short hair!" This is how pervasive and ingrained the myth of the short-haired lesbian is, that even while long-haired lesbians feel invisible and unrecognized as lesbians by other lesbians, they, too, fall prey to the assumptions that the short-haired woman they meet is more likely to be a lesbian than the woman whose hair is long.

HETEROSEXUALS' PERCEPTIONS OF LONG-HAIRED LESBIANS

Long-haired lesbians are often perceived by heterosexuals as heterosexual and/or as "available" to men, due in part to a perception many men have that if a woman is attractive (i.e., she possesses some of their images of beauty, like long hair), she couldn't possibly be a lesbian. Lisa said that men have a hard time believing that she's gay because of her appearance: "I had a guy hit on me. He knows I'm a lesbian, he's like, you're so cute, and your hair's so pretty. . . . And I said, that doesn't make any difference, I'm still gay. I had to convince him." These perceptions are often seen by other lesbians as an ability to "pass," to fit in, to move easily and closeted among the mainstream dominant culture. Long-haired lesbians are perceived as buying into and perpetuating male-generated images and standards of beauty. This is a double standard, because lesbians who shave their legs and underarms, or pierce their ears, or take on any number of other supposedly "male-defined" standards of beauty are rarely accused of "buying in" to the extent that lesbians with long hair are.

On the other hand, long-haired lesbians challenge many of the stereotypes about how lesbians are supposed to look (i.e., "like men"). Some find that their appearance can be useful, and they take satisfaction in breaking these stereotypes. Kippy noted, "I think it's really good for people to learn that lesbians are people, not a static image, that lesbians are individuals, and that there are lesbians that can be who they are, and not conform to some sort of societal dictates." And Lisa pointed out that her looks help put heterosexual people at ease, and make it easier for them to talk with her and find out more about her life: "I'm not exactly the butch poster child for lesbians, but I think I'm very approachable and I have people ask me a lot of questions. They're curious . . . that's been very helpful, and I think having long hair helps [make her approachable]."

However, it can be just as frustrating for lesbians to remain unrecognized for who they are by the heterosexual world as it is to be unrecognized in their own communities. As Susan put it, "I think straight people think all lesbians look like butch style lesbians, [with] short hair . . . and they forget about us. The invisible lesbians." As a result, both in the lesbian communities and in the mainstream, many long-haired lesbians make an effort to identify themselves in some way: dressing more "butchy," wearing rainbow hoops or a labyris. As Taica said, "Every time I go to Northampton I'm like, oh damn, I forgot to wear my pink triangle, or my rainbow rings. I'm always bummed that I'm not wearing something to identify me."

WHY THE MYTH OF THE SHORT-HAIRED LESBIAN PERSISTS

The women I interviewed identified a number of reasons for the predominance of short hair and the dismissal of long hair among lesbians. For one, we all make stereotypes and assumptions, and short hair as the lesbian flag has been accepted for a long time. As Emily described, it's also human nature to divide, label, and categorize people and things, often in a dualistic way:

> Humans like to divide and label things, that's part of the way we process our experiences, we try to figure out patterns. It's a survival mechanism: are these people threats, are these people friends, are these predators or prey? . . . Our society has done a lot of almost arbitrary binary divisions, men are this way, and women are this way. . . . Within the lesbian community we do the same thing. We, lesbians, are like this, as opposed to straight women are like that. Butches are like this, femmes are like this. Short-haired lesbians are like this, long-haired are like that.

Taica further explained the issue of safety:

> I think that it's not real safe for us to assume that somebody's a lesbian unless we really, really know. In the way that I dress and the way that I wear my hair, I'm not displaying any of the cultural cues we've set up to tip each other off, so they can't be sure unless I have on a pink triangle or rainbow rings around my neck or something. And it's not safe to give that look to straight women. So I think lesbians tend to be pretty cautious, unless they really know that they're dealing with another lesbian.

For many lesbians, the rejection of long hair, along with other examples of feminine "beauty," is a rejection of the traditional expectations of and limitations on women, as well as an adamant desire not to be perceived as supporting or "buying into" those stereotypes. As Taica stated, "Women have historically been expected to have long hair, that's how the societal standard of beauty has been described. Long hair was part of the standard of beauty that we were expected to live up to." Emily further described these limitations:

> [There is a] constricting image of femininity that in some ways I represent because I have longer hair. Femininity gets shoved down all of our throats, all our lives. I think especially as little girls we're really drilled about conforming to this feminine standard. . . . Sometimes [short-haired lesbians'] anger at society and society's constrictions about women gets directed at us [long-haired lesbians].

Emily also pointed out that long-haired lesbians become the brunt of some lesbians' anger because they are perceived as being able to pass and fit in with the heterosexual world, both in the present, and in the past: the "girlie" girl child who had it easier than the tomboy:

> I think that that experience [of being like a boy] is much more painful than what I had. I mean, I never felt like I was feminine enough, but people never labeled me masculine either. A lot of lesbians as little girls got labeled in really hurtful ways, and really felt excluded.

Chris also talked about being perceived as passing as heterosexual, based on appearances: "We put values on a certain look, and there may be some value judgment around women who are completely passable, because they're so feminine. They have long hair and are not putting forth any obvious lesbian-type signs." Again, this idea that long-haired lesbians "are not putting forth any obvious lesbian-type signs" implies that the "obvious" lesbian has short hair.

In discussing the anger directed at those lesbians who can pass from those who can't, Susan compared it to the issue of skin color:

> It's this straight privilege thing . . . I can walk through the mall and go to the women's restroom, I don't get a lot of problems, I can move easily among straight people . . . [A] woman talked to me about being angry at long-haired lesbians because they could pass for straight; she's a butch dyke and looks like a man to a lot of straight men and women, and she's got this anger at me, because I'm femmy. . . . Sort of like in African-American communities where the really light-skinned African-American people can "pass" for white . . . and how angering that is to people who feel like they can't pass.

Finally, for Kippy this bias against long-haired lesbians and other expressions of femininity stems from "a very deep seated fear of people being individuals and expressing their true selves . . . I think there might be people who are really scared of androgyny or scared of their feminine side or scared of being who they are and letting down their guards."

THE FEMME-BUTCH CONNECTION
AND THE REJECTION OF THE FEMININE

There is a connection between hair length and femme-butch images and stereotypes. Though there are definitely exceptions, a general assumption exists that if one has longer hair, she is a femme, and if one has very short hair, she's more butch. (Of course, there are butch lesbians with long hair, but other lesbians rarely perceive them as heterosexual.) Further, a sense has developed in the lesbian community that to be butch is preferable to being femme, an example of how some lesbians have internalized the sexist messages that male is better than female. Maureen used dancing as an example of how lesbians seem to be more interested in and find it more desirable to lead than to follow: "I think it's a male-identified thing that following is worse than leading, that to be empowered is to only be leading." As Susan further explained:

> [They] make it sound like if you're competent with tools or can fix things or are good at sports then you're butch. So if you're incompetent and helpless, then you're a femme? . . . I think there is this value on being butch that it's sort of like men and women, like feminine and masculine, like masculine is supposedly better, like God forbid you call a man a woman by accident. I think a lot of butches get insulted if you say that they're somewhat femmy.

Emily has felt this emphasis on the butch in the form of hostility directed towards her at a lesbian gathering:

> I was really the only long-haired lesbian there and I felt kind of under attack. My girlfriend and this other woman were talking about how they didn't like to go camping, and no one said anything until I piped up and said I didn't like camping either, and then all these people, like turned on me, oh the femme, she doesn't like camping! This is very interesting that these two women who might on that kind of dichotomy be described as butch, nobody made any comments about them, but I felt like there was some hostility directed in my direction.

One of the women at this party had earlier made a comment about having been "such a boy" when she was younger. Emily continued:

> She said it with great pride. And if you said, oh, I was such a girl, it doesn't carry the same kind of pride, people look at that like, oh, girlie. . . . There is something there about real rejection of things feminine. We were presented and continue to be presented with such a narrow, narrow idea of what women are, that we've rejected that out of hand, and you're presented with a very wide ranging, almost all encompassing view of what it means to be a man. . . . So I think that instead of rejecting that dichotomy and that socially constructed sort of approach, I think that people have in some ways accepted that and rejected the feminine.

We need only look back to our own childhood, as Chris explained, to understand some of these attitudes: "That goes way back to my childhood, growing up with all boys and boys having more privileges and being treated better in general."

Being butch has often been identified with being lesbian. Because of this emphasis on the non-feminine, short-haired look, many lesbians do not see themselves reflected in the lesbian community. Based on the images of lesbians they saw, a number of women figured that was not who they were. This further raises the question of how many feminine lesbians don't come out because they only see images of butch women as lesbians, as Emily described her own experience:

> There is a kind of a lesbian look, and the main component of that is having very short hair. . . . I was a month shy of 30 when I came out. I think part of my problem as to why it took me so long to come out is, I had lesbian friends, but they all seemed so different from me. I was never a jock, I wasn't really a tomboy, and I wasn't into what on the surface it seems a lot of people in the lesbian community are into. I think if I had known more lesbians, like this group of long-haired lesbians, that it might have made me challenge my assumptions about myself a lot earlier.

CONCLUSIONS

A number of myths and misperceptions related to images of lesbian beauty surround hair length. Although a growing number of lesbians are choosing to keep their hair long, or to grow it long again, rather than succumb to the pressures of cutting it to achieve the "Dyke Look," long-haired lesbians are often still unrecognized as lesbians among both lesbians and heterosexuals.

The long-haired lesbians I interviewed spoke of the assumptions and stereotypes that all lesbians have short hair, and of the perceived pressures and expectations that lesbians should cut their hair when they come out. They felt invisible as lesbians, even marginalized by other lesbians, based on their hair length. Further, they expressed that heterosexuals not only did not recognize them as lesbians, but often assumed they were straight out of a belief that if they were attractive by men's standards, how could they possibly be lesbians?

These women discussed this rejection of long hair as one result of a general rejection of traditional images of the feminine and the concomitant limitations that are forced upon them. At the same time, perhaps contradictorily so, is the greater emphasis and importance placed upon the masculine, which translates into greater importance on the more butch characteristics, including short hair. While not wanting to embrace the constraining traps of femininity and rejecting those "male-defined" standards of beauty, women overlook the fact that, as Maureen pointed out, while "feminine" is male-defined, "masculine" is also male-defined. Either way, lesbians seem to be basing their standards on those of the male-dominated mainstream society.

And, by incorporating these standards and rejecting the inherent feminine, lesbians have internalized the very sexist beliefs of the dominant culture that they attempt to reject in the first place. Even in rejecting these images, women are held captive by them.

Whereas having such identifying "flags" as short hair has been useful in the past, as more different kinds of women are coming out as lesbian, it is necessary to avoid making assumptions based on a woman's hair length or other aspects of appearance. The time has come to create our own images of who and what lesbians are and can be, and of our definitions of lesbian "beauty." A lot more lesbians may find long hair attractive than are admitting it. The time has come for us to look at other ways of being. After all, that is part of what being a lesbian is all about. Emily's words offer an eloquent summary:

> There's no reason that women's hair should symbolize oppression or be chained to heterosexuality or be chained to men or anything like that. Look at how men's long hair in the Bible symbolized strength and power. . . . The secret thing is how many women with really short hair have come up to me and said they wished that they had the guts to grow their hair long. . . . In some very real way, that's what lesbianism is about, choices and alternatives to any kind of mainstream imperative. We want to have choices to be and do and look like whatever we want, as long as you're not hurting anyone else, that's what it's about. And so I think short haircuts, buzz haircuts, shaved heads, hair down to your toes, frizzed hair, straight hair, whatever! . . . And if that's the only way we're recognizing each other is by our haircuts, then we're doing something wrong.

Even My Hair Won't Grow Straight

Ellen Samuels

SUMMARY. The author narrates the experience of growing her hair long after years of keeping it short, and ponders the "the socioculturo-sexual implications of hair growth." While her lesbian friends respond with curiosity and doubt, the rest of the world, including her grandmother, wants to see long hair as a return to traditional (straight) femininity. *[Article copies available for a fee from The Haworth Document Delivery Service: 1-800-342-9678. E-mail address: getinfo@haworthpressinc.com]*

The day I start sleeping with Becca, I decide to grow my hair long again. I've tired of the lesbian chic aesthetic which dictates that I sport a hairstyle oddly similar to that of boys my mother brought home in 1955. At lunch the next day, I declare my intention to an admiring circle of friends around a family-sized table at the Peking restaurant, while wolfing down fried chicken wings and Chunking pork.

"Aren't you afraid no one will recognize you?" asks my roommate, whose background in psychology enables her to focus immediately on the social impact of my decision while I'm still debating its aesthetics. Her question panics me: Will dykes in other towns still meet my eyes in that

Ellen Samuels received her Master of Fine Arts degree in creative writing from Cornell University. Her poetry and articles have appeared in *The American Voice, Sojourner, The Lesbian Review of Books*, and *The Journal of the American Medical Association*, among others. She has been awarded a 1997 grant by the Constance Saltonstall Foundation for the Arts.

Address correspondence to: Ellen Samuels, 1 Mead Street #3, Somerville, MA 02144.

[Haworth co-indexing entry note]: "Even My Hair Won't Grow Straight." Samuels, Ellen. Co-published simultaneously in *Journal of Lesbian Studies* (The Haworth Press, Inc.) Vol. 3, No. 4, 1999, pp. 103-105; and: *Lesbians, Levis and Lipstick: The Meaning of Beauty in Our Lives* (ed: Jeanine C. Cogan and Joanie M. Erickson) The Haworth Press, Inc., 1999, pp. 103-105; and: *Lesbians, Levis and Lipstick: The Meaning of Beauty in Our Lives* (ed: Jeanine C. Cogan and Joanie M. Erickson) Harrington Park Press, an imprint of The Haworth Press, Inc., 1999, pp. 103-105. Single or multiple copies of this article are available for a fee from The Haworth Document Delivery Service [1-800-342-9678, 9:00 a.m. - 5:00 p.m. (EST). E-mail address: getinfo@haworthpressinc.com].

103

meaningful, I know you from someplace, Bogart-to-Bergman moment I so relish? I haven't even considered that growing my hair could mean becoming less visible as a lesbian–if anything, I thought it might make the huge "L" tattooed on my forehead even more noticeable when I pulled my bangs back in one of those nifty stiff-pleated combs.

I just want my hair back–my hair that I know will burst from its sculpted cap into curls that appear to turn corners, right-angling out from my temples like brown periscopes. When I had hair that took three hours to dry and covered my breasts in a Lady Godiva-esque curtain, people used to touch it all the time. They brushed it, braided it, simply lifted long strands and let them fall, riffling into multitudes of separate and reckless threads. When I cut my hair off, it wasn't primarily to signal coming out; it was a means of pulling back from the world, denying that tactile access I'd come to find overwhelming. There's something clarified, controllable, *clean-cut*, about having short hair. When the hair began to test its boundaries, to creep down my scalp or over my ears, I simply called for the clippers: "Size-three guard. Even it out in back." So what if my hair still grew exuberantly, necessitating frequent trips to the hairdresser? What I spent on trims I saved on trimming–I only had to buy shampoo twice a year.

Now that I'm letting the hair have its way, though, everything changes. I have to purchase a blow dryer, special conditioner to counteract the blow dryer's impact, hair spray to make that impact last, and barrettes for when the hair spray fails (usually about ten minutes after leaving the bathroom). With all the new chemicals I'm applying to my scalp, I develop an allergy, huge red pimples reminiscent of junior high cropping up on my forehead. So I buy acne medication. It's no lie that cultural expectations of female beauty are designed to hit us hardest in the pocket book–or the fanny pack, depending on taste. But as a dyke, I feel both under-invested in the beauty culture rat race–*who cares if my bangs don't stay in place*–and overly insecure–*can everyone tell I haven't touched a blow dryer since high school*? Finally, there's that uneasy feeling that, willingly or not, I'm buying back into a system I rejected so long ago that it no longer seemed to be an issue.

Too bad my grandma knows better. At Christmas she asks if my hair has changed. *It sure has*, I reply. *I'm growing it long again.* Oh, she answers calmly, getting up to put the orange juice back in the refrigerator. *So . . . are you still gay?* Oh, Grandma. You've never studied psychology and even you know I can't escape the socioculturosexual implications of my hair growth. So why am I in such denial? Maybe it's because I've refused, defused, and deconstructed the "feminine" equation of appearance and identity so thoroughly that I thought I'd attained a kind of second Eden, a socially-pure vacuum in which I could shape my personal aesthetic to meet only my own needs and requirements.

Or maybe there's a deeper reason. I'm secretly trying to recuperate the boons I used to receive for looking like a "girl": the reverent fingers teasing through my hair, the admiring glances at my mini-skirted legs, the cozy chats with my girl cousins about mascara thickness and staying power. Maybe it was seeing Becca in her ankle-brushing black nylon nightgown that reignited my own latent desire for softness, silkiness, and *length*. As I struggled to slide the tight ebony bodice over her breasts, it occurred to me that I used to own a lot of black lace accouterments myself. Where were they? At the Salvation Army in Oberlin, Ohio, abandoned when I finished college? Stuffed in the bottom of my underwear drawer, stifled by wool socks and Jockey-for-Her? When had I stopped dressing up sexy for dates, and hadn't it been *fun*?

My friend Jaclyn would say this moment of realization signaled the acceptance of my femme identity, my coming-of-age as a lipstick lesbian who knows you can love women and still prefer Victoria's Secret over The Gap. But honestly, I had short hair for years, and no one, not even Grandma, accused me of being butch. Cropped or coiffured, I still project enough femme mystique to be the cover girl for the next Joan Nestle anthology. It's something about the way I run, the way I giggle, the way I scream when large dogs race at me barking their lungs out–just as my friend Nina, whose hair cascades past her shoulders, can't walk into a room without being pegged as the jock she is. Maybe hair length can be a determinant of identity at a certain liminal stage–say, the "baby dyke" phase–but it soon becomes apparent that we cannot rely upon the scalp-to-tip ratio to guide our mating radar. Finger-nail length might be a more accurate identificatory trait, but can you imagine asking that hot short-haired woman in the grocery check-out line to remove her gloves for a moment?

I do narcissistically appreciate the attention that comes as my hair lengthens and becomes a separate entity, rather than a mere extension of myself, something to be noticed and discussed in public–rather like a dog or a baby. Does this mean I'm buying back into a stereotype of womanhood, sidling back into the closet, or otherwise selling out? I hope not, as I love the way my hair feels in the shower as I massage the shampoo through its weight, at night as it rests between my cheek and pillow, its lush sensuality daily enticing me to put off the hairdresser's appointment, let it grow just a little more, make it last just a little longer. If anything, my newfound romance with my hair suggests new erotic possibilities–I find myself checking out long-haired women at the mall or in waiting rooms, wondering if we have more in common now that my hair looks more like theirs than their fourteen-year-old son's; if maybe we have more in common than I ever realized.

Beauty and the Butch

Bonnie Ruth Strickland

SUMMARY. This personal narrative describes the reactions of a "butch" lesbian to notions of "beauty." I grew up in a Southern culture that glorifies strength, courage, and honor for males and beauty, care-taking, and passivity for females. My interests and activities in childhood were almost exclusively masculine. Beauty was of little importance to me except as a characteristic of the desired other. Through adolescence and young adulthood I felt alienated, confused, and conflicted about sexuality, gender, and beauty. I lived my personal and professional lives independently of each other. As I grew older and as social attitudes changed, I eventually began to incorporate and integrate a more complete and complex sense of being. *[Article copies available for a fee from The Haworth Document Delivery Service: 1-800-342-9678. E-mail address: getinfo@ haworthpressinc.com]*

Bonnie Ruth Strickland was raised in the South and received her PhD in clinical psychology from the Ohio State University in 1962. She has been on the faculties of Emory University and the University of Massachusetts at Amherst as teacher, researcher, administrator, clinician, and consultant. She has been President of the American Psychological Association, the Division of Clinical Psychology and the American Association of Applied and Preventive Psychology. She was a founder of the American Psychological Society. A long-time advocate for women and minorities, she serves on numerous boards and committees and has presented testimony before the United States Congress. She has published more than 100 scholarly works and has two Citation Classics. She lives on a lake in the Pioneer Valley with her three cats and her Chocolate Labrador, Murphy Brown.

Address correspondence to: Bonnie R. Strickland, PhD, Department of Psychology, University of Massachusetts, Amherst, MA 01003-7710.

[Haworth co-indexing entry note]: "Beauty and the Butch." Strickland, Bonnie Ruth. Co-published simultaneously in *Journal of Lesbian Studies* (The Haworth Press, Inc.) Vol. 3, No. 4, 1999, pp. 107-115; and: *Lesbians, Levis and Lipstick: The Meaning of Beauty in Our Lives* (ed: Jeanine C. Cogan and Joanie M. Erickson) The Haworth Press, Inc., 1999, pp. 107-115; and: *Lesbians, Levis and Lipstick: The Meaning of Beauty in Our Lives* (ed: Jeanine C. Cogan and Joanie M. Erickson) Harrington Park Press, an imprint of The Haworth Press, Inc., 1999, pp. 107-115. Single or multiple copies of this article are available for a fee from The Haworth Document Delivery Service [1-800-342-9678, 9:00 a.m. - 5:00 p.m. (EST). E-mail address: getinfo@haworthpressinc.com].

My mother was, and is, a beautiful woman who loves men. My father was handsome and loved women. When they met at a summer party in 1934 it was love at first sight; they married three weeks later. Eventually, I came along although not without some resistance. My mother was in labor with me for a duration of time that gets longer each time she tells the story. Finally, the physician, using forceps that distorted my skull and left vascular birthmarks on my face, pulled me, reluctant and unbreathing, into this world. After being plunged first into hot water and then cold–the highest technology of 1936–I began to cry. My mother says that she awoke to see me, red and ugly, in my father's arms. She asked "What is it?" and my father lovingly said "It's a baby girl." My mother remarked that she knew how much my father had wanted a boy; he replied "I didn't know she was going to be so pretty." Well, pretty I was not and I've always been confused about beauty–mine, not other people's. But, there is no doubt that my mom and my delusional dad thought they took home a pretty baby girl and treated me as such.

My young mother dressed me and my favorite dolls in frilly clothes, some of which she made herself. She held my hand when we walked outside and comforted me when I was frightened of the airplanes that flew overhead (there weren't many in the late 1930s). She would lie down beside me when I took a nap and let me twine my tiny fingers through her hair. At age 80, she still eagerly and unbidden shows off my baby pictures–a sometimes solemn but usually smiling child with a ribbon in her hair, a bracelet on her arm, and a ring tied to her middle finger. No doubt, when the visitors are gone and as she puts the pictures away, my mother looks at them longingly, wondering what happened to that beautiful baby girl these last 60 years.

The first grandchild of my father's family who lived in Birmingham, Alabama, I was doted on by my grandfather and my two uncles. When we visited the northwest Florida swamps of my mother's family, I was one of innumerable grandchildren (I think there were close to 50), constantly parented by aunts, uncles, and cousins. As far as I know all of them fit proudly and securely into their heterosexual roles. The men were handsome and pleased to provide for the beautiful women they pursued. The women embraced every aspect of femininity, dressing fashionably and leaning lovingly on the strong arms of their men. Only with their brothers and their closest kin would they ever betray the reality of handling a shotgun or slopping the hogs as well as any man. The men and women of my Southern family modeled clear gender roles in which women were beautiful and sexually charming; and men adored them.

Like other American children of the 1940s, and every generation before and after, I assumed that I had a choice of only two sex roles. I could follow the dictates of my assigned gender as a girl and be assimilated into the social structures of beauty, fashion, and femininity. Or, I could follow the dictates of my heart and act, feel, and think like a boy–active, independent, strong. No difficult decision here. On the Florida rivers, I learned to fish and shoot a rifle. In the streets of Birmingham, I climbed rooftops and played competitive games, always with boys as my preferred playmates. I wanted nothing to do with conventional notions of being female. Beauty felt completely foreign to me. My interests and ideals were bravery, independence, and strength. If I had thought about it, I would have realized that women can be courageous and strong, but I had fallen into a Southern (and American) culture that rewarded boys and men for what were considered important activities, like war, and girls and women for being soft and fluffy and taking care of others. With the simplicity of childhood, I chose boyhood.

Passing as a boy would not have been that difficult except for such crisis-generating handicaps as having long hair and wearing dresses (girls in the 1940s did not wear pants except for one rebellious day in the eighth grade when we were all sent home from school). Moreover, my mother insisted that I take piano lessons. The lessons weren't that bad–I pounded out much frustration on our well-worn upright–and I knew that boys sometimes played the piano (although not any self-respecting boy that I knew from my working-class neighborhood). But, the piano recitals were my undoing. Having memorized a piece to play for the proud and smiling parents in an overheated church basement, I would clumsily make my way on stage wearing a dress with my hair in long curls–rather like I dressed for church at Easter except with a piano instead of a preacher. The frilly frock exposed me as a girl–weak, someone who would kowtow to boys rather than winning at their games or beating them up, no longer their equal in courage, honor, and strength.

The ardor of my parent's love at first sight had faded with a second look and they divorced when I was 7. My mother took a job and, luckily for me, was not around during the day to continually push her notions of femininity. Growing up, I never thought much about beauty. I knew that being a boy and being beautiful was an oxymoron so I assumed that being a "butch" girl and being beautiful was equally absurd. I was intent on body building and becoming a good athlete. I considered the wisdom of "kissing my elbow and turning into the opposite sex." I really didn't think this would work but I almost broke my arm trying. I spent hours admiring ads for body-building, especially the Charles Atlas portrayal of a strong muscle-bound male kicking sand on the blanket of a beautiful young woman while her skinny escort looks on in dismay. He then takes a Charles Atlas course, improving his physique and besting the villain when he returns. I tried hard to build my own muscles but, unfortunately, when I looked in the mirror, my scrawny chest and pitiful biceps were more those of the helpless skinny escort than the newly remade hero. But, at least I didn't look like the helpless woman in the picture.

Did I really want to be a boy? I don't know. I simply remember that for as long as I can recall of my growing-up days, I preferred boy type activities and from an early age knew that my romantic interests were girls. Like the Atlas ads, all of my fantasy heroes were male, usually sports figures. I spent days in our backyard pretending to sink the winning, championship basket in front of the roaring crowds. It was not me standing in the driveway and hitting a tennis ball against the side of the house but Bill Tilden on center court at Wimbledon; I was Joe Louis pounding away at a punching bag swinging under our back porch. I was a good athlete, usually among the first chosen for our pick-up games. I felt strong and confident; I knew how to take care of myself and was generally fearless.

Adopting a masculine persona also meant that I should not have any feelings at all and never talk about my innermost thoughts unless they were the expected male-type conversations. I easily fell into discussions about heavy weight boxing, major league baseball, and our beloved minor league Birmingham Barons. I knew the batting averages of each player and the earned run stats for every pitcher. I could hold forth indefinitely on the horsepower, styling, and fuel requirements of any late model car. Falling back on my Florida adventures, I could talk endlessly about the relative merits of shotguns versus rifles for killing almost any creature and I always knew the perfect rod and bait for fishing. I never mentioned my confusion about my gender or my deep frustrations of being treated as a girl. If I did find beauty around me, it was in the perfect bunt laid down to advance a runner to second base or floating with my fantasies in the sun dappled swamp of my mother's family homeland. Conventional notions of feminine beauty were completely foreign, and even frightening, to me. Once when I had to deliver a phone message to my mother at a neighborhood beauty shop, I stood at the door in an absolute panic. All courage left me when I was faced with having to walk into women's space with the scent of shampoo and the heat of hair dryers. I dashed in, delivered the message, and frantically escaped back into the fresh air, frightened, perhaps, by the glimpse of my future when I would be a grown-up woman. It would be years before I would feel comfortable in a beauty parlor; or a place where women took care of one another. I was in my fifties before I had a massage.

Although my outdoor adventures would occasionally lead to scrapes and bruises, I never cried and refused to admit pain. I was so stoic that one summer when I fell and cut my hand on some cinders, I never mentioned the swelling or the red marks that were running up my arm. My mother heard me cry out in my sleep and took me to the family doctor who lanced the wound and immediately sent me to the hospital. I was there for a week and the heat was unbearable (there was no air conditioning in those days). A student nurse noticed my discomfort and wiped my shoulders and back with alcohol. Except for my brother and I punching each other, we had never been very demonstrative in my family. I summoned up my courage and asked if she would return sometime and she came back the next several days and rubbed my back. I began to think there might be something to this "expressing feelings" stuff and I had a new respect for "touching."

As I entered my teens, my mother frantically escalated her efforts at a gender change–mine, not hers. She did *not* share my excitement at having been named center of the 90 pound YMCA boys' football team. In fact, she refused to allow me to play with boys any longer. Being an enterprising youngster, I simply wandered from the football fields in the park across the street from our house to the softball diamonds. No doubt, my mother would have joyfully reconsidered her decision had she known that I had found a lesbian softball team. These women wore pants, sharpened their cleats, and were as good at brawling as they were at playing ball. Most folks would have looked on this field and seen more brawn than beauty–no Southern belles in this line-up. But these women were beautiful to me. I was at home where women dressed as they pleased and found joy in their play and each other. They let me sit on the bench with them and keep score; they laughed a lot and tousled my hair. The first baseman gave me a baseball cap with the team name emblazoned across the front. I only took it off when I went to bed. I still have it, packed away with the memories of strong women, who I now know were also beautiful, who by opening their hearts to me, opened mine.

When I attended an all-women's college, another group of beautiful, strong women invited me into yet another community, one more of the mind than the body. Faculty women comprised every aspect of teaching, research, and scholarship and expected us students to do the same. We were all involved in student government, designing the residence hall regulations under which we lived, and taking responsibility for our behavior. I was captain of some of our intramural sports teams, elected Recreation Director, and an announcer on our campus radio station. But, the role I played best was that of the male, romantic lead in our theater productions.

Acting served me well in college, and beyond. Usually I was content with my gym clothes, starched white shirt and shorts under a rain coat (we could not wear shorts or pants to classes). But, occasionally, like the dreadful piano recitals of my childhood, I would don an evening gown for a college formal, my sunburned neck and tan arms outlined by my gym shirt giving mute testimony to my real life.

In an attempt to socialize us rural, working-class, and small-town girls, young officers in training from various military bases were occasionally bussed to the college in their most elaborate dress uniforms for parties and a dance. Since I had been recently the recipient of not one but two evening dresses (which my mother bought me in her continuing efforts at my gender transformation), for the first time I signed up for an escort for the dance. I dressed and waited patiently (not easy for me) for my "date" to arrive, watching from the window of my dorm room as handsome young military men appeared to meet their woman of the evening. No one came for me. I had humiliated myself by signing up for this frigging dance, painted my face, and decked myself out in a formal, only to sit unwanted and rejected in a dark window. I tried to see the irony of having finally decided to sign up for an escort and having my name misplaced. I could not muster up either a sense of humor or righteous anger. Instead, this kid who never cried, sat in the dark with hot tears staining a lacy evening dress that I had never wanted to wear in the first place.

During my junior year, my college, faced with dire financial contingencies, admitted male students to improve revenues. It had never occurred to me that men were essential or necessary in the life of the college; I preferred bankruptcy. Bringing men into our bucolic existence was not nearly as disruptive as I expected. In fact, I became one of the guys, roaming the country side, swimming in the rivers, and exploring caves and old mines that had played out years before. I enjoyed the physical strength of the men and their willingness to take risks. Although we had no name for our comradery, perhaps there was a kind of social beauty in our reliance on each other. I knew that I could count on rescue if I mis-stepped on a mountain or ventured too far in a swift current. But, like the young men with whom I shared adventure, I, too, thought primarily of beauty as belonging to the other–beautiful women, those soft feminine creatures to whom I was so attracted.

When I completed the busy work of graduate school and took a job in the academy, life became more complicated. Like most minorities, I had to make a place for myself in two worlds. I could live on the margins or I could move between my personal and private lives, playing with male gusto on my feminist softball team or going to social events on the arm of a man (usually a handsome, charming, gay man). My partner's picture was never on my work desk and my professional colleagues seldom met my personal friends. No doubt, many of my department faculty suspected that I was lesbian and would have welcomed my coming out to them. But, it was not safe to admit one's homosexuality in the 1950s and 1960s. Police routinely raided not only gay bars but private parties where lesbians might gather. I would have been fired from my faculty position as were a number of gay men at my university who were inadvertently "outed."

So, I transgressed boundaries and lived across cultures, never letting people in the straight world see me at home in the lesbian community, or vice versa. A bi-racial friend of mine has written extensively about the relationship of slaves to their master in those cruel days of slavery. She remarks that there is "One self for my master to see; one self that I know is me" (Jeanette Miller, personal communication). This was certainly true for me as I presented myself as womanly and heterosexual in the dominant culture but lived as a butch lesbian with my close friends and lovers. I recall one instance, in particular, when I became painfully aware of my clash of "selves." The Dean of Women at my university resigned unexpectedly (to join the Peace Corp, at age 55) and the administration was desperately looking for a replacement. I was 27 years old and one of the only female faculty on campus. In spite of the fact that I had always avoided deans of any kind and knew nothing of their responsibilities, I was offered and took the position. Within a few months, I was interviewed by a local reporter. Among the many questions she asked was if I had occasion to counsel unwed mothers. I innocently responded that actually several unwed fathers had come by in the last few weeks to talk about their problems. The photographer took a few pictures of me in my office; the reporter said the story would be published soon, and they left.

The following Sunday morning, I brought in the *Atlanta Constitution* and blazoned across the bottom of the front page were the headlines "Dean of Women Sees Unwed Fathers." Inside was one of the sexiest pictures I have ever seen, a smiling, even beautiful young woman sitting in a chair, hair styled, legs crossed with skirt above her knee–and it was me. I couldn't believe it. I kept looking at the picture, sometimes looking away, and then looking back. Who was this person with my name in the caption? I called the reporter complaining that the story and the cheesecake photo misrepresented everything I believed about myself and my job. Too late. The Associated Press had picked up the story–which made the front page, with picture, in major newspapers across the country and internationally. I received hundreds of letters, numerous requests for dates, and five marriage proposals. Every unwed father in the world seemed to want to talk with me. Looking back, I wish I could have just enjoyed the ensuing publicity, incorporating whatever of myself was feminine and beautiful into a more total picture. But, I was surprised and hurt, believing that the attractive, smiling woman of the picture was the false front of a serious, masculine being who had no business masquerading as a female.

And, so it was. I lived a double life, sometimes passing in the straight world but more often living closeted in the gay life. One public self represented my assigned sex, female, very occasionally beautiful, and sometimes romantically attracted to men. The other was my real self, masculine, attracted by female beauty, and desirous of the intimacy, the closeness, and the warmth of women. I always dated beautiful women–that's what Southern gentlemen did–and I eventually settled into a traditional Southern marriage. I was the provider and some twenty-five years ago, my lovely partner left her professional position to follow me on a job move to a university in the dreaded North. To our surprise, as Southerners and lesbians, we were warmly welcomed into a faculty family of supportive friends and colleagues. We found a home in both our personal and professional worlds. We played softball on a feminist team comprised predominantly of lesbians at the same time that we played on the straight teams at the University. We attended school socials of heterosexuals and gave a Fourth of July party attended by, perhaps, the largest gathering of lesbians in the Northeast at that time. I eventually began to teach Lesbian Psychology, affectionately called Dyke Psych.

My partner kept a lovely home, entertained splendidly, and was the traditional help-mate in my adventures. She always had a luscious meal on the table when I came home from work and I wasn't allowed in the kitchen. I loved being married; I had always known that I would rather have a wife than be one. But living as the stereotypical couple with all the inequities of traditional sex roles was a large component of our deciding to separate after eighteen years.

With freedom at fifty, I began to explore all sorts of new adventures and see all kinds of interesting women, one of whom was an elegant and glamorous woman from Colorado. She was a tall, blond, respected professional with a stunning mountain home. An occasional model for department stores and designers, she loved dressing for the opera, for outdoor concerts, for visits to Telluride or Taos and she wanted me to dress up when she took me along. We wore designer clothes on the ski slopes and every head would turn when we–perhaps I should say she, with me tagging along–walked into a restaurant. We were seated at the best tables and pampered by adoring waiters. Once, on a trip in her new convertible to her condo in Vail, we were traveling through a mountain pass without having seen a car for miles. The engine began to overheat and she pulled to the side of the road. I was just about to bound out of the car to take a look when from nowhere, I mean from absolutely nowhere since we could have been stranded on the arctic tundra, a handsome, smiling policeman appeared and quickly knocked the snow off the radiator. Men were always materializing to help her out and me too if I was along (and properly dressed). For the first time in my life, I began to enjoy wearing make-up, having my hair styled, and dressing in fashionable clothes.

Coming out is a continual process that never ends but I have gradually begun to feel open to letting people know me across whatever aspects they think important. I have a rich network of lesbian friends–including some of the softball team members of over 40 years ago–but, at this time of my life many of my closest friends are straight men and women. I still wear jeans and hiking boots but I also enjoy dressing up whether for a Lesbian Tea dance or a university social. I think of myself more as transgendered than as male, female, or lesbian and have finally come to live comfortably across my different selves, my different families, and my different communities. One of my faculty colleagues talked of watching his three-year-old daughter primp and preen in front of a mirror while wearing her favorite frilly pink dress and her fairy princess angel wings. She kept admiring herself and proudly repeating, "I am beautiful." He then watched her flex her tiny biceps as she looked approvingly at her image and heard her further announce, "I am beautiful and I am strong." At age 60, I finally know what she means.

Why has an acceptance and integration of my being (which may never be finished) taken so long and been so difficult? What imperatives force us to adopt bi-polar sex roles? Who ever decreed that human beings could be only male or female? And, whatever the etiology of sex roles, why don't we change a phenomenon that is so damaging to both men and women and all of us in between? As each of us tries desperately to make our way in this world, we are constantly surrounded by those institutionalized mores and language that keep us less than we could be. Among its many definitions, beauty is most often feminine, defined by softness and pleasant curves, and brings women to mind. Couldn't our understanding of beauty and all of those other sex-linked words be expanded and creatively incorporated to more accurately describe the fullness of our being? Freedom. I am talking about freedom and there is no more beautiful word in the English language.

PART III

COMPULSORY THINNESS: ARE LESBIANS IMMUNE FROM THE BARBIE MANDATE?

i used to stuff it with potato chips, bowls of
pasta and half pints of ben and jerry's
ice cream at the end was necessary
it numbed the throat and offered a slide
for the chips and pasta to easily follow
out the same door they entered

see you can have your cake and eat it too–those fools who write proverbs
though my dentist never noticed the enamel on my teeth was rotting

excerpt from a poem (see pp. 119-120)
written by a lesbian, recovered from bulimia
now happily loving her body

Secret Torrent

Jeanine C. Cogan

it builds like a wave
dependably growing, gaining force,
showing off its crest like a peacock preening
it gets too large and folds in on itself
crashing to the shore
against sand, skeleton shells, and water crabs that
are too small for eating
all the underworld life is churned up
and as the crescendo comes to a close
like a changed record, or a second thought,
the water is calmly drawn backward
over the chaos and disarray

it spins like a top, though not creating a beautiful
blur of colors that forms a pattern as the
top slows in speed
it spins rather like a child methodically turning
herself in circles just because it's fun
but she becomes dizzy and sick
falls to the floor and is stunned
each time she is stunned yet continues to turn
herself in circles continues to become dizzy, sick
and fall

[Haworth co-indexing entry note]: "Secret Torrent." Cogan, Jeanine C. Co-published simultaneously in *Journal of Lesbian Studies* (The Haworth Press, Inc.) Vol. 3, No. 4, 1999, pp. 119-120; and: *Lesbians, Levis and Lipstick: The Meaning of Beauty in Our Lives* (ed: Jeanine C. Cogan and Joanie M. Erickson) The Haworth Press, Inc., 1999, pp. 119-120; and: *Lesbians, Levis and Lipstick: The Meaning of Beauty in Our Lives* (ed: Jeanine C. Cogan and Joanie M. Erickson) Harrington Park Press, an imprint of The Haworth Press, Inc., 1999, pp. 119-120. Single or multiple copies of this article are available for a fee from The Haworth Document Delivery Service [1-800-342-9678, 9:00 a.m. - 5:00 p.m. (EST). E-mail address: getinfo@haworthpressinc.com].

i used to stuff it with potato chips, bowls of pasta
and half pints of ben and jerry's
ice cream at the end was necessary
it numbed the throat and offered a slide
for the chips and pasta to easily follow
out the same door they entered

see you can have your cake and eat it too–those
fools who write proverbs
though my dentist never noticed the enamel on my
teeth was rotting

other times i would lose myself to her flesh
as she laid her head on my arm and shoulder
one breast firmly against my chest, and her right
leg draped over my legs and abdomen
her hand caressing mine
i would pull her closer and closer, nuzzle my head
against hers and kiss her gently
even if it was for just a moment
even if the sharing of our bodies was all we shared
i'm good at living for moments
it's all i ever really know i have anyway

now i hide from it with my friends
we dine together, watch the latest of hollywood on
swollen screens, with
music that fucks our every emotion
we buy a seat among hundreds of other seats with
people in them we do not talk to, sometimes look
at but never will see again
and park in a parking lot with so many cars we
write down the number or letter that corresponds
to our particular spot

and always i come home again
it is just me
alone
and the wave inside starts to
build, the top begins to spin
and i fall and am
stunned

Lesbians and the Internalization of Societal Standards of Weight and Appearance

Karen Heffernan

SUMMARY. Findings from a study of body image, weight concern, and disordered eating in lesbians are presented. While lesbians were more critical of traditional social norms regarding the rights and roles of women in general than heterosexual controls, this difference disappeared in regard to norms concerning women's weight and appearance. Dieting was frequent, almost half of the participants were dissatisfied with their weight, and self-esteem was strongly influenced by body esteem. A large number of lesbians said that physical attractiveness was important in a partner. However, lesbians' conception of physical attractiveness had a more functional quality, related to physical condition, and less concern for conventional aspects related to "looks" than heterosexual women. Involvement in lesbian, but not feminist, activities was

Karen Heffernan, PhD, is currently Associate Director of the Anxiety and Traumatic Stress Programs at the Payne Whitney Clinic, New York Hospital-Cornell Medical Center, where she is engaged in clinical and research work with survivors of childhood abuse. She completed her graduate work at Rutgers University, New Jersey, where she was coordinator of the Eating Disorders Clinic. She has published articles in the area of eating disorders, and the relationship between sexual orientation and eating disorders, and was the recipient of the 1995 *Lesbian Psychologies Unpublished Manuscript Research Award* of the Association for Women in Psychology. This article is based on the author's master's thesis and doctoral dissertation.

Address correspondence to: Karen Heffernan, PhD, Payne Whitney Clinic, New York Hospital-Cornell Medical Center, 525 East 68th Street, Box 147, New York, NY 10021 (E-mail: kheffern%pw@nyh.med.cornell.edu).

[Haworth co-indexing entry note]: "Lesbians and the Internalization of Societal Standards of Weight and Appearance." Heffernan, Karen. Co-published simultaneously in *Journal of Lesbian Studies* (The Haworth Press, Inc.) Vol. 3, No. 4, 1999, pp. 121-127; and: *Lesbians, Levis and Lipstick: The Meaning of Beauty in Our Lives* (ed: Jeanine C. Cogan and Joanie M. Erickson) The Haworth Press, Inc., 1999, pp. 121-127; and: *Lesbians, Levis and Lipstick: The Meaning of Beauty in Our Lives* (ed: Jeanine C. Cogan and Joanie M. Erickson) Harrington Park Press, an imprint of The Haworth Press, Inc., 1999, pp. 121-127. Single or multiple copies of this article are available for a fee from The Haworth Document Delivery Service [1-800-342-9678, 9:00 a.m. - 5:00 p.m. (EST). E-mail address: getinfo@haworthpressinc.com].

121

found to be a protective factor against low body esteem. These findings are discussed in terms of understanding lesbians' relationships to beauty norms, variations across subgroups, and risk for eating problems. *[Article copies available for a fee from The Haworth Document Delivery Service: 1-800-342-9678. E-mail address: getinfo@haworthpressinc.com]*

Do lesbians internalize traditional beauty norms to a lesser degree than heterosexual women, translating into reduced risk for body dissatisfaction and eating disorders? Or are they equally vulnerable, or vulnerable in different ways?

Claims that lesbians are less invested in conventional norms of attractiveness received some empirical support from a 1983 survey of American couples. Only 35% of lesbian respondents rated the physical attractiveness of a partner as important, telling the researchers "time and again . . . that conventional standards of female beauty ultimately did not matter to them" (Blumstein & Schwartz, 1983, p. 250). In contrast, 67% of cohabiting and 57% of married heterosexual males rated physical attractiveness of a partner as important–a finding that is consistent with other studies that have found men to place more emphasis on physical appearance in evaluation of potential romantic partners than do women.[1] If male valuing of appearance plays a part in heterosexual women's concern about their looks, then women who choose other women as partners may be subject to less pressure with regard to their physical attractiveness.

In fact, the pressure may go in the opposite direction. Among many lesbians dieting and stigmatization of fat women is socially unacceptable because it is seen as 'buying into' oppressive societal norms of female appearance and behavior (Schoenfielder & Wieser, 1983). If, as Brown (1987) and others suggest, lesbians are more likely to view stigmatization of fat women as oppression, there may be support for fat women to accept their body size and less pressure to diet.

An alternative hypothesis, however, is that lesbians are no less susceptible to body dissatisfaction than heterosexual women. We do not know how many women with eating disorders are lesbian because openness regarding this has not been socially encouraged, and few studies have asked. Dworkin (1989) and others argue that lesbians, growing up in the same culture and equally subject to its messages concerning thinness and attractiveness, show the same discontent with their bodies and preoccupation with dieting.

A study by Striegel-Moore et al. (1990)[2] offers support for this second hypothesis. No significant differences were found on measures of body esteem and disordered eating between a small sample of lesbian and heterosexual college students. The authors concluded that the critical stance of lesbians toward cultural ideals regarding women may not be sufficient to supplant already internalized beliefs and values. The study also examined the relationship between body esteem and self-esteem to explore the purported deemphasis of appearance by lesbians, and found that the link between self-esteem and body esteem was in fact stronger among the lesbians. In particular, physical condition (agility, stamina and strength) was significantly related to self-esteem in the lesbians only, reflecting, the authors suggest, an emphasis on physical strength within lesbian culture.

While Siever (1994) found less vulnerability to body dissatisfaction among lesbians and heterosexual men than among gay men and heterosexual women, a study by Brand, Rothblum, and Solomon (1992) found greater body dissatisfaction, perceived overweight and dieting among the women, regardless of sexual orientation. However, while the lesbians and gay men in this study tended to weigh more than the heterosexual subjects, they did not perceive themselves to be overweight any more than the latter. Lesbians also reported less extreme ideal weights than heterosexual women.

Finally, in a study by Herzog, Newman, Yeh and Warshaw (1992), participants selected figure drawings to represent their current and ideal figures, the figure they felt would be most attractive to a potential partner, and the figure to which they themselves would be most attracted. There was a significantly wider gap between current and ideal figure, higher weight concern, and more dieting among the heterosexual women than among lesbians, even though, as a group, the lesbians weighed more. In addition, the figures chosen by lesbians to represent what they felt would be attractive to another and to themselves, tended to be heavier than those of heterosexual women. However, while these differences were significant, the authors point out that more than 40% of the women in both groups felt overweight, wanted to lose weight, and experienced daily concern about their appearance–suggesting again the common vulnerability of all women.

CURRENT STUDY

A central question not addressed by the studies reviewed is the extent to which the lesbians in their samples were critical of social norms: Do lesbians reject societal standards of beauty for women? Lesbians are no less heterogeneous than heterosexual women–some do not claim a lesbian identity, some do so only socially, while others are identified with lesbian and/or feminist activism (Golden, 1987; Oldham, Farnill, & Ball, 1982)–and it cannot be assumed that all lesbians equally reject or accept these societal norms.

This was explored in a study that aimed to move beyond comparison of group differences between lesbians with heterosexual women, and to explore the different factors that may affect body image, weight concern and eating disorders among lesbians (Heffernan, 1996).[3] Two hundred sixty-three lesbians, and a control group of heterosexual women, completed the Attitudes

Toward Women Scale (ATWS: Spence & Helmreich, 1978), which assesses endorsement of statements pertaining to the roles, rights and privileges of women in general, and the Attitudes Toward Attractiveness Scale (ATAS: Rodin, Striegel-Moore, & Silbertstein, 1985). The ATAS assesses the degree to which women endorse sociocultural norms regarding thinness and attractiveness, as expressed in statements such as, "It is impossible for a heavy person to look as attractive as a thin person," and "overweight people should be ashamed of 'letting themselves go.' "

LESBIANS' ATTITUDES ABOUT WEIGHT AND APPEARANCE

A striking finding emerged from these measures. Lesbians were significantly more critical of traditional attitudes regarding the rights and roles of women in general than the heterosexual control group, but this difference disappeared on the Attitudes Toward Attractiveness Scale (ATAS), suggesting that this critical stance does not extend to matters of weight and appearance. Furthermore, the higher the internalization of these beauty norms, the higher the degree of weight and shape concern among respondents.

LESBIANS AND DIETING

The findings of this study strongly suggested that it is a misperception that dieting is infrequent among lesbians. There is a perception that lesbians view dieting as being socially unacceptable and "oppressive," yet 48% of the lesbians in this study reported engaging in it on at least half the days during the previous 3 months, suggesting that a tension may exist between the publicly held mores of the lesbian community and the private realm of preoccupation and discontent. It may be that this tension makes it even more difficult for a lesbian to acknowledge that she has body image problems, and may contribute to what Brown (1987) and Thompson (1992) have referred to as a particular stigma among lesbians regarding eating disorders.

The study also found that almost half of the participants were at least moderately dissatisfied with their weight (this was replicated in a later study, Heffernan, 1997), and self-esteem was strongly influenced by body esteem.[4] And, as body weight increased, so did the discrepancy between participants' actual and ideal weights; the greater respondents' weight, the greater their degree of weight concern, and the lower their body esteem. In a follow-up study, Heffernan (1997) also found that lesbian participants scored higher on an inventory measuring dietary restraint, weight and shape concern and dissatisfaction, than similar individuals in the general population. It would seem that lesbians are not protected from the discontent generated by thin standards of female beauty.

BUFFERING FACTORS

There were significant differences in degree of weight concern between those who were and were not considerably involved in lesbian/gay activities, suggesting that there may be some "buffering" effects of being actively involved in and exposed to other lesbian and gay persons. There was also some influence on shape concern and dieting. Perhaps being around others who are like oneself, where one can be openly lesbian, contributes to self-ascceptance. It is equally likely that lesbians who are out, and already self-accepting, are more likely to be involved in lesbian/gay identified activities.

Interestingly, unlike some other research findings (see this volume), there was no such relationship between these measures and involvement in feminist activities. What accounts for these different findings is unclear and warrants further research.

PHYSICAL ATTRACTIVENESS AND PARTNER SELECTION

An unexpectedly high proportion (63%) of the lesbians in this study said that the physical attractiveness of a partner was important to them. Again, this is contrary to popular conception, and to Blumstein and Schwartz's (1983) findings. Perhaps their interviews elicited a social desirability effect that was not present in the anonymous self-report questionnaire used in the present study. It may also reflect a shift in the 13 years between 1983 and 1996. However, another possibility is that what lesbians mean by physical attractiveness is different from conventional notions of female beauty, as was indicated by the number of respondents who noted in the margins of this question a distinction between what is conventionally considered attractive and what is attractive to them.

This possibility is supported by the findings on a measure assessing physical characteristics that influenced respondents' evaluation of potential romantic partners. On this scale, they rated how important each of 35 aspects of physical appearance and functioning was in their evaluation of another woman's physical attractivess. The scale has 3 subscales. The first subscale, "sexual attractiveness," includes items primarily related to facial features conventionally associated with female physical attractiveness, and items related to sexuality (e.g., cheekbones, lips, breasts). The second subscale, "weight," includes body parts defined as those that can be altered through dietary restriction or exercise (e.g., hips, thighs, stomach, waist). The third subscale, "physical condition," includes items pertaining to agility, coordination, stamina, strength and energy level. It was the latter subscale that emerged as the most salient in lesbians' evaluation of partners, suggesting that their conception of physical attractiveness has a more functional quality, and less concern for conventional aspects related to "looks."

In summary, research to date suggests that lesbians' alternative lifestyle may not be sufficient to undo the effects of growing up in a culture that conveys to females from an early age that what is most valued is their looks. However, there are indications that lesbians do differ from heterosexual women in a number of ways. Weight was rated as being the least important aspect of a partner's attractiveness, which may mean lesbians are under less pressure at least from partners to meet a thin beauty mandate. The findings concerning degree of involvement in lesbian/gay activities suggest that lesbians may begin to look more different from heterosexual women the more identified they are with lesbian/gay culture. Future research on the mechanisms at work here, and on the relationships between self-acceptance, internalized homophobia and body esteem, would be beneficial.

NOTES

1. See Heffernan (1996) for references not included here and below, for sake of brevity.
2. See Heffernan (1994) for critique of the studies reviewed here.
3. See Heffernan (1996) for a full description of the sample, method, measures, and results.
4. Satisfaction with various aspects of physical appearance and functioning.

REFERENCES

Blumstein, P., & Schwartz, P. (1983). *American couples: Money, work and sex.* New York: William Morrow.

Brand, P.A., Rothblum, E.D., & Solomon, L.J. (1992). A comparison of lesbians, gay men, and heterosexuals on weight and restrained eating. *International Journal of Eating Disorders, 11*, 253-259.

Brown, L. (1987). Lesbians, weight and eating: New analyses and perspectives. In Boston Lesbian Psychologies Collective (Eds.), *Lesbian Psychologies: Explorations and challenges* (pp. 294-309). Chicago: University of Illinois Press.

Dworkin, S.H. (1989). Not in man's image: Lesbians and the cultural oppression of body image. *Women and Therapy, 8*, 27-39.

Golden, C. (1987). Diversity and variability in women's sexual identities. In Boston Lesbian Psychologies Collective (Eds.), *Lesbian Psychologies: Explorations and challenges* (pp. 18-34). Chicago: University of Illinois Press.

Heffernan, K. (1994). Sexual orientation as a factor in risk for binge eating and bulimia nervosa: A review. *International Journal of Eating Disorders, 16,* 335-347.

Heffernan, K. (1996). Eating disorders and weight concern among lesbians. *International Journal of Eating Disorders, 19,* 127-138.

Heffernan, K. (1997). Binge eating, coping, and affect regulation among lesbians. Manuscript submitted for publication.

Herzog, D.B., Newman, K.L., Yeh, C.J., & Warshaw, M. (1992). Body image satisfaction in homosexual and heterosexual women. *International Journal of Eating Disorders, 11,* 391-396.

Oldham, S., Farnill, D., & Ball, I. (1982). Sex-role identity of female homosexuals. *Journal of Homosexuality, 8,* 41-46.

Rodin, J., Striegel-Moore, R.H., & Silberstein, L.R. (1985). Attitudes Towards Attractiveness Scale. Unpublished scale.

Schoenfelder, L., & Wieser, B. (Eds.) (1983). *Shadow on a tightrope: Writings by women on fat oppression.* Iowa City: Aunt Lute Book Co.

Siever, M. (1994). Sexual orientation and gender as factors in socioculturally acquired vulnerability to body dissatisfaction and eating disorders. *Journal of Consulting and Clinical Psychology, 62,* 252-260.

Spence, J.T., & Helmreich, R.L. (1978). *Masculinity and femininity: Their psychological dimensions, correlates, and antecedents.* Austin: University of Texas Press.

Striegel-Moore, R.H., Tucker, N., & Hsu, J. (1990). Body image dissatisfaction and disordered eating in lesbian college students. *International Journal of Eating Disorders, 9,* 493-500.

Thompson, B.W. (1992). "A way outa no way": Eating problems among African-American, Latina, and White women. *Gender and Society, 6,* 546-561.

Body Image, Compulsory Heterosexuality, and Internalized Homophobia

Gayle E. Pitman

SUMMARY. Body dissatisfaction in lesbians is a subject which has traditionally been ignored in the psychological literature on body image and eating disorders. Early feminist theorists and researchers argued that body dissatisfaction in women developed as a way of dealing with the oppression and misogyny they are faced with on a daily basis. However, these theories failed to take issues of race, class, and sexual orientation into account, thereby excluding the experiences of a diversity of women. This article focuses specifically on the lesbian experience and explores how cultural messages about thinness, femininity, and heterosexuality shape lesbians' feelings about their sexuality and about their bodies. Through the inevitable process of internalizing homophobia and fat hatred, both of which are institutionalized ways of keeping heterosexuality

Gayle E. Pitman, MA, earned her doctoral degree from the California School of Professional Psychology-Alameda. Her dissertation research is on the relationship between body dissatisfaction and internalized homophobia in lesbians. Her interests include the etiology of eating disorders from a feminist and sociocultural perspective, power and gender issues in rape, sexual assault, and childhood sexual abuse, and feminist issues in psychological testing.

Address correspondence to: Gayle E. Pitman, California School of Professional Psychology-Alameda, 1005 Atlantic Avenue, Alameda, CA 94501.

The author would like to thank Valory Mitchell, Kristin Hancock, Jeanine Cogan, Nancy Hoopes, and Anne Rodriguez for their feedback, suggestions, and support, all of which were very helpful in articulating her ideas. She also thanks Jeanine Cogan for her enthusiasm surrounding the author's dissertation and for encouraging the writing of this article. Finally, the author would like to thank Nancy Hoopes and Elizabeth Guzik for their helpful editorial comments.

[Haworth co-indexing entry note]: "Body Image, Compulsory Heterosexuality, and Internalized Homophobia." Pitman, Gayle E. Co-published simultaneously in *Journal of Lesbian Studies* (The Haworth Press, Inc.) Vol. 3, No. 4, 1999, pp. 129-139; and: *Lesbians, Levis and Lipstick: The Meaning of Beauty in Our Lives* (ed: Jeanine C. Cogan and Joanie M. Erickson) The Haworth Press, Inc., 1999, pp. 129-139; and: *Lesbians, Levis and Lipstick: The Meaning of Beauty in Our Lives* (ed: Jeanine C. Cogan and Joanie M. Erickson) Harrington Park Press, an imprint of The Haworth Press, Inc., 1999, pp. 129-139. Single or multiple copies of this article are available for a fee from The Haworth Document Delivery Service [1-800-342-9678, 9:00 a.m. - 5:00 p.m. (EST). E-mail address: getinfo@haworthpressinc.com].

and female oppression in place, lesbians may begin to believe that there is something inherently wrong with them and with their bodies. This article explores how the impact of racism, classism, sexism, and homophobia on women may provide a more comprehensive understanding of the cultural forces behind women's dissatisfaction with their bodies. *[Article copies available for a fee from The Haworth Document Delivery Service: 1-800-342-9678. E-mail address: getinfo@haworthpressinc.com]*

Feminists have traditionally focused on gender role conflict, cultural misogyny, and female oppression in constructing a sociocultural theory of the etiology of body dissatisfaction, weight preoccupation, and eating disorders in women. These theories arose from feminist arguments that body dissatisfaction and eating disorders in women are a manifestation of the oppression they experience in a culture in which they are devalued and disempowered. However, while female oppression is certainly a component of women's global dissatisfaction with their bodies, many of the theories have not taken issues of race, class, and sexual orientation into account. In fact, until recently the literature on body image disturbance and eating disorders has completely excluded lesbians, women of color, and working-class women, despite the fact that women in all of these groups are pressured in our society to be thin (Root, 1990; Striegel-Moore, Tucker, and Hsu, 1990; Thompson, 1994).

This paper will present a cultural theory of body image disturbance with regard to the lesbian experience. The central focus will be upon the oppressiveness of dominant white heterosexual culture, citing the female body as the vehicle through which culturally prescribed messages about femininity, beauty, and heterosexuality are inscribed. From this perspective, I theorize that the cluster of forces socializing women towards heterosexuality are the same cultural forces that socialize women to be thin, forces which serve to disempower the lesbian experience and privilege heterosexuality and thinness.

RESEARCH ON LESBIANS AND BODY IMAGE: FINDINGS AND FLAWS

The majority of studies on body dissatisfaction and eating disorders in women of color and in lesbians have yielded comparative data to heterosexual Caucasian women. In general, this research indicated that upper-middle-class heterosexual Caucasian women are more likely than women of color or lesbians to harbor a negative body image (Brand, Rothblum, and Solomon, 1992; Harris, 1994; Herzog, Newman, Yeh and Warshaw, 1992; Lucero et al., 1992; Parker et al., 1995; Rosen et al., 1991; Rucker and Cash, 1992; Siever,

1994). In interpreting these results, some researchers put forth the theory that the thin ideal of dominant white heterosexual culture may not be the ideal for other groups. For example, Herzog et al. (1992) suggest that lesbians as a group may be more satisfied with their bodies and idealize a heavier weight than heterosexual women. This phenomenon may occur because lesbians may be more likely to be aware of the sexism shrouded within cultural ideals of beauty and, therefore, are less likely to subscribe to them.

Unfortunately, a common interpretation is that lesbians, working-class women, and women of color are somehow insulated from dominant white culture and that issues of body dissatisfaction and eating disorders are not relevant to these women. In fact, several recent studies have shown just the opposite: that lesbians are more likely than men or almost as likely as heterosexual women to be dissatisfied with their bodies or to have symptoms of an eating disorder (Beren, Hayden, Wilfley & Grilo, 1996; Brand et al., 1992; Heffernan, 1996; Striegel-Moore et al., 1990). Two important issues arise with respect to studies which compare one group to another. First, extreme differences between the two groups tend to obscure the very presence of the studied trait or behavior within each group. In this case, the finding that upper-middle class white heterosexual women tend to feel less comfortable with their bodies and are more likely to be preoccupied with their weight and appearance than lesbians, working-class women, or women of color obscures the fact that body dissatisfaction and eating disorders are phenomena common to all women, regardless of race, class, or sexual orientation. Second, studies which yield no difference between two groups that are being compared are generally not published. By not appropriately paying attention to the incidence of body dissatisfaction and eating disorders in lesbians, working-class women and women of color, however low this may be, we lose the opportunity to explore within a global cultural context why these difficulties might occur.

Because of these exclusions, the above theories of body dissatisfaction and eating disorders have focused solely on the politics of gender without considering the impact of other forms of oppression in our culture. It is therefore necessary to construct a more comprehensive, multifaceted theory which incorporates issues of race, class, and sexual orientation, as well as issues of gender, in order to explore more fully why eating and body image disturbances are so pervasive in our culture.

Some theorists have already begun to focus on the presence of eating disorders and body dissatisfaction in women of color. For example, Osvald and Sodowsky (1993) theorized that acculturation to white Western society through the internalization of media images, racism, and messages regarding gender role, as well as a rise in socioeconomic status, all co-occur with the internalization of the white Western concept of beauty and thinness. As a result, women of color cope with their feelings of internalized racism by harboring negative feelings about their bodies. Recent studies with African-American, Asian-American, and Latina women generally support this theory (Abrams, Allen and Gray, 1993; Akan and Grilo, 1995; Harris, 1995; Lopez, Blix and Blix, 1995; Makkar and Strube, 1995; Thompson, 1994). For example, Latina, African-American, and white women interviewed in Thompson's (1994) study described how their eating problems and dissatisfaction with their bodies arose in part as survival strategies against injustices such as racism, classism, sexism, homophobia, and the stress of acculturation.

Lesbians may go through a similar process of cultural internalization. The following section presents a conceptualization of body dissatisfaction in lesbians as impacted by dominant white heterosexual culture, specifically through the mechanisms of compulsory heterosexuality and the internalization of homophobia.[1]

COMPULSORY HETEROSEXUALITY
AND INTERNALIZED HOMOPHOBIA

Women of all race, class, and sexual identities are exposed to and to some extent internalize cultural messages concerning gender and the female body. In a similar manner, all women who live in our culture are overtly and subtly socialized to become heterosexual. Adrienne Rich (1980) coined the term "compulsory heterosexuality" to describe "the cluster of forces [in Western society] by which women have been convinced that marriage, and sexual orientation toward men, are inevitable, even if unsatisfying or oppressive components of their lives" (p. 12). All of our societal institutions, including the family, religion, government, schools, and mass media, are constructed around the ideal of compulsory heterosexuality. Examples of how compulsory heterosexuality is enforced include family pressures to marry by a certain age, social events geared towards heterosexual couples, and the various economic benefits associated with heterosexual marriage.

One of the ways women and men are convinced of innate heterosexuality is through the homophobia present in individuals and in society. The term "homophobia" was first defined by Weinberg (1972) to mean "the irrational fear, hatred, and intolerance of homosexual men and women." Since then, the definition of homophobia has been expanded and used to explain how negative images of lesbians and gay men are promoted and reinforced in our culture. At the same time, in light of the fact that homophobia is inevitable in a society whose foundation is built upon oppression and prejudice against lesbians and gay men, many scholars have challenged the notion of homophobia as an "irrational" belief system (Kitzinger, 1996).

Morin and Garfinkle (1978) define homophobia as:

any belief system which supports negative myths and stereotypes about homosexual people. More specifically, it can be used to describe (a) belief systems which hold that discrimination on the basis of sexual orientation is justifiable, (b) the use of language or slang, e.g., "queer," which is offensive to gay people, and/or (c) any belief system which does not value homosexual life styles equally with heterosexual life styles. (p. 30)

These belief systems are adopted and promoted in society and its institutions to ensure that heterosexuality is kept in place. The institutional promotion of homophobia is manifested through every aspect of our culture, including the prohibition of same-sex marriages; the limited portrayal of gay and lesbian characters on TV, movies, and advertisements; the prohibition of same-sex couples at school dances, formals, and other social events; and churches being forced to exclude gay men and lesbians from their congregations. In fact, this homonegativity is so pervasive in our society that it is impossible to avoid internalizing these homophobic attitudes on a personal level.

Shidlo (1994) defines "internalized homophobia" as "a set of negative attitudes and affects toward homosexuality in other persons and toward homosexual features in oneself, including same-gender sexual and affectional feelings, same-gender sexual behavior, same-gender intimate relationships, and self-labeling as lesbian, gay, or homosexual" (p. 178). Internalized homophobia includes not only conscious negative attitudes toward homosexuality but also unconscious beliefs and feelings. Both conscious and unconscious internalized homophobia can be expressed in a myriad of ways, including fear of discovery; discomfort with obvious "fags" and "dykes"; rejection and denigration of all heterosexuals; feeling superior to heterosexuals; beliefs that lesbians are not different from heterosexual women; an uneasiness with children being raised in a lesbian home; restricting attraction to unavailable women, heterosexual women, or those already partnered; and short-term relationships (Margolies, Becker, and Jackson-Brewer, 1987).

In fact, the internalization of homophobia is viewed as a normative developmental event, whereby all gay men and lesbians incorporate negative attitudes toward homosexuality early in their developmental history (Shidlo, 1994). Through the internalization of societal homophobia, lesbians and gay men begin to believe that there is something inherently wrong with them, rather than seeing the prejudicial and discriminative forces at work that promote and reinforce the heterosexism in our culture.

Many writers have hypothesized that internalized homophobia has a major impact on the psychological development of lesbians and gay men. Most of the data on gay men suggest that internalized homophobia is correlated with depression and low self-esteem (Alexander, 1986; Shidlo, 1994), HIV status (Ross and Rosser, 1996), relationship dissatisfaction (Ross and Rosser,

1996), avoidant coping (Folkman, Lazarus, Dunkel-Schetter, DeLongis and Gruen, 1986), somatic symptoms, loneliness, and distrust (Shidlo, 1994).

While several studies have been conducted on the effects of internalized homophobia on gay men, relatively few studies have looked at how internalized homophobia affects lesbians. Although many of the above findings are probably true for lesbians as well, researchers have theorized that homophobia in our culture manifests itself within the individual psychology of lesbians as sexual dysfunction (Brown, 1986), relationship difficulties (Cleff, 1994; Downey and Friedman, 1995), depression (Rothblum, 1990), and weight preoccupation (Brown, 1987). This last phenomenon, the notion of weight preoccupation and body dissatisfaction resulting from cultural and internalized homophobia, will be developed further in the following section.

BODY IMAGE, COMPULSORY HETEROSEXUALITY, AND INTERNALIZED HOMOPHOBIA

> A lesbian, closeted on her job because of heterosexist prejudice, is not simply forced into denying the truth of her outside relationships or private life; her job depends on her pretending to be not merely heterosexual but a heterosexual *woman*, in terms of dressing and playing the feminine, deferential role required of "real" women. (Rich, 1980, p. 642)

In the above passage, Adrienne Rich (1980) describes how lesbian women are expected to conform to the norms of femininity and heterosexuality through their outward appearance. The concept of culture being expressed through our individual bodies is one of the central tenets of the work of Michel Foucault, a French poststructuralist philosopher who postulated the theory of the body as a cultural text. According to Foucault and other poststructuralist philosophers, gender, sexuality, race, and other identities are culturally defined constructs which change over time and which shape our physical appearance, thereby rendering our bodies as representations of the culture in which we live (McNay, 1992).

Susan Bordo (1993), a feminist contemporary of Foucault, expanded upon his theory of body as text and focused more specifically upon the female body. According to Bordo, in terms of gender socialization, messages about femininity and heterosexuality become imprinted upon the female body in the form of the cultural ideal of female beauty. The slender ideal toward which women strive in our culture is a physical manifestation of those feminine characteristics women are taught to value, including weakness, passivity, and claiming as little physical space as possible (Bordo, 1993). These cultural notions of female beauty arise from a fat-oppressive belief system so pervasive that all women internalize these attitudes on an individual level to some degree. As a result of internalizing aspects of this belief system, women may begin to dislike their own bodies, harbor a negative body image, and at the extreme, develop symptoms of an eating disorder.

Just as the slender ideal promotes and upholds a sexist belief system, fat oppression is but one agent that reinforces heterosexism in our society. However, little emphasis has been given to how lesbians are affected by these societal messages, despite the fact that an overwhelming amount of literature exists regarding the sexist implications of cultural prescriptions of physical appearance on women. While lesbians as a group may have different norms for physical appearance, lesbians, like all women, are consumers of mass culture and are also subjected to cultural ideals of female beauty (Rothblum, 1994). All women in our culture are subjected to fat hatred, just as all women in our culture are subjected to homophobia (Brown, 1987). Embedded within these cultural lessons about thinness are messages concerning femininity and heterosexuality, and thus both sets of cultural belief systems are often instilled simultaneously. For example, many women are taught that being slender and attractive will help them "to catch a man and be assured of economic survival" (Dworkin, 1988, p. 29). As a result, women internalize the importance of stylizing themselves into desirable objects for work opportunities and for marital happiness and security. Incorporating messages such as these into one's personal belief system may have a particularly strong impact on lesbians, a multiply stigmatized group.

The conjunction of fat oppression and homophobia within our culture is quite evident in the extremely negative attitudes promoted within dominant culture regarding the physical appearance of lesbians. Rothblum's (1994) compilation of research findings indicates that lesbianism is often equated with unattractiveness, and that lesbians are more liked and accepted by others when their appearance conforms with feminine and heterosexual standards. The homophobia inherent in these common stereotypes serves to promote and reinforce compulsory heterosexuality by linking acceptance and sexuality with appearance and size; i.e., by attributing positive characteristics to thinness and heterosexuality and negative characteristics to lesbianism and fatness. As a result of internalizing these attitudes, lesbians may feel just as pressured as heterosexual women to conform to cultural ideals of beauty as well as to society's rules concerning heterosexuality to gain acceptance within society at large.

At the same time, lesbians get the implicit message that violating these societal rules may have stunning consequences. Laura Brown (1987), in her analogy between the internalization of fat hatred and the internalization of homophobia, illustrates the implications of challenging the dominant cultural belief system:

A woman who nurtures herself with food, and who does so without guilt, shame, and self-hate has challenged a very basic message given women against feeling worthy of love and sustenance. A lesbian who loves herself and her love of other women and does so without guilt, shame, and self-hate breaks another such rule, that of compulsory heterosexuality. A woman who is spending time and energy on her own pleasure by feeding herself lovingly, by using the resources available to her, by taking as much space as her body grows into, is as clearly revolutionary as is the woman who loves, values, and commits her energies to the love of women. (p. 301)

Brown's (1987) analogy between the internalization of fat hatred and the internalization of sexism and homophobia points to a connection between these two cultural forces. While fat oppression clearly reinforces the sexism that is ever-present in our culture, it also operates on a deeper level to promote the notion of compulsory heterosexuality. The overall message that fat oppression conveys is that women's bodies are unworthy, undesirable, and unlovable, a message which serves to undermine women's love for other women as well as for themselves. Clearly, lesbians who are comfortable with their bodies and with their sexuality are violating the rules of dominant white heterosexual culture, a culture which has been structured to keep women of all identities in a devalued and disempowered position.

NOTE

1. A number of scholars have criticized the use of the terms *homophobia* and *internalized homophobia*, arguing that these terms depoliticize lesbian and gay oppression and suggest that the individual is at fault for holding these beliefs (i.e., see Kitzinger, 1996). To stress the fact that the internalization of this prejudice is due to a system of political and institutional oppression in our society, many scholars have chosen to use the terms *heterosexism, cultural heterosexism,* and *psychological heterosexism.* In this article, I argue that homophobia is instilled in lesbians and gay men on an individual level in order to uphold the complex system of heterosexist oppression within our culture at large. Thus, I have chosen to use the terms homophobia and internalized homophobia, define them without any assumptions of individual pathology, and illustrate how the internalization of homophobia is inevitable and in fact reflects a pathological society rather than a pathological individual.

REFERENCES

Abrams, K.K., Allen, L., and Gray, J.J. (1993). Disordered eating attitudes and behaviors, psychological adjustment, and ethnic identity: A comparison of Black and White female college students. *International Journal of Eating Disorders, 14(1),* 49-57.

Akan, G.E. and Grilo, C.M. (1995). Sociocultural influences on eating attitudes and behaviors, body image, and psychological functioning: A comparison of African-American, Asian-American, and Caucasian college women. *International Journal of Eating Disorders, 18(2)*, 181-187.

Alexander, R.A. (1986). *The relationship between internalized homophobia and depression and low self-esteem in gay men.* Unpublished doctoral dissertation, University of California at Santa Barbara.

Beren, S., Hayden, H.A., Wilfley, D.E., and Grilo, C.M. (1996). The influence of sexual orientation on body dissatisfaction in adult men and women. *International Journal of Eating Disorders, 20(2)*, 135-141.

Bordo, S. (1993). *Unbearable Weight: Feminism, Western Culture, and the Body.* Berkeley: University of California Press.

Brand, P.A., Rothblum, E.D., and Solomon, L.J. (1992). A comparison of lesbians, gay men, and heterosexuals on weight and restrained eating. *International Journal of Eating Disorders, 11(3)*, 253-259.

Brown, L.S. (1986). Confronting internalized oppression in sex therapy with lesbians. *Journal of Homosexuality, 12*, 99-107.

Brown, L.S. (1987). Lesbians, weight, and eating: New analyses and perspectives. In the Boston Lesbian Psychologies Collective (Eds.). *Lesbian Psychologies* (pp. 294-309). Urbana: University of Illinois Press.

Cleff, B.G. (1994). *The relationship between internalized homophobia, coping efforts and relationship satisfaction in lesbians.* Unpublished doctoral dissertation, University of Nevada, Reno.

Downey, J.I. and Friedman, R.C. (1995). Internalized homophobia in lesbian relationships. *Journal of the American Academy of Psychoanalysis, 23(3)*, 435-447.

Dworkin, S. (1988). Not in man's image: Lesbians and the cultural oppression of body image. *Women and Therapy, 8(1-2)*, 27-39.

Folkman, S., Lazarus, R.S., Dunkel-Schetter, C., DeLongis, A., and Gruen, R.J. (1986). Dynamics of a stressful encounter: Cognitive appraisal, coping, and encounter outcomes. *Journal of Personality and Social Psychology, 50*, 992-1003.

Harris, S.M. (1994). Racial differences in predictors of college women's body image attitudes. *Women and Health, 21(4)*, 89-104.

Harris, S.M. (1995). Family, self, and sociocultural contributions to body image attitudes of African-American women. *Psychology of Women Quarterly, 19(1)*, 129-145.

Heffernan, K. (1996). Eating disorders and weight concern among lesbians. *International Journal of Eating Disorders, 19(2)*, 127-138.

Herzog, D.B., Newman, K.L., Yeh, C.J., and Warshaw, M. (1992). Body image satisfaction in homosexual and heterosexual women. *International Journal of Eating Disorders, 11(4)*, 391-396.

Kitzinger, C. (1996). Speaking of oppression: Psychology, politics, and the language of power. In Rothblum, E.D. and Bond, L.A. (Eds.). *Preventing Heterosexism and Homophobia* (pp. 3-19). Thousand Oaks: Sage Publications.

Lopez, E., Blix, G.G. and Blix, A.G. (1995). Body image of Latinas compared to body image of non-Latina White women. *Health Values: The Journal of Health Behavior, Education and Promotion, 19(6)*, 3-10.

Lucero, K., Hicks, R.A, Bramlette, J. & Brassington, G.S. (1992). Frequency of eating problems among Asian and Caucasian college women. *Psychological Reports, 71(1),* 255-258.

Makkar, J.K. and Strube, M.J. (1995). Black women's self-perceptions of attractiveness following exposure to White versus Black beauty standards: The moderating role of racial identity and self-esteem. *Journal of Applied Social Psychology, 25(17),* 1547-1566.

Margolies, L., Becker, M., and Jackson-Brewer, K. (1987). Internalized homophobia: Identifying and treating the oppressor within. In Boston Lesbian Psychologies Collective (Ed.). *Lesbian Psychologies* (pp. 229-241). Urbana: University of Illinois Press.

McNay, L. (1992). *Foucault and Feminism.* Boston: Northeastern University Press.

Morin, S.F., and Garfinkle, E.M. (1978). Male homophobia. *Journal of Social Issues, 34,* 29-47.

Osvald, L.L. and Sodowsky, G.R. (1993). Eating disorders of White American, racial and ethnic minority American, and international women. *Journal of Multicultural Counseling and Development, 21(3),* 143-154.

Parker, S., Nichter, M., Nichter, M., & Vuckovic, N. (1995). Body image and weight concerns among African-American and White adolescent females: Differences that make a difference. *Human Organization, 54(2),* 103-114.

Rich, A. (1980). Compulsory heterosexuality and lesbian existence. *Signs: Journal of Women in Culture and Society, 5(4),* 631-660.

Root, M.P. (1990). Disordered eating in women of color. *Sex Roles, 22(7-8),* 525-536.

Rosen, E.F., Anthony, D.L., Booker, K.M., & Brown, T.L. (1991). A comparison of eating disorder scores among African-American and White college females. *Bulletin of the Psychonomic Society, 29(1),* 65-66.

Ross, M.W. and Rosser, B.R.S. (1996). Measurement and correlates of internalized homophobia: A factor analytic study. *Journal of Clinical Psychology, 52(1),* 15-21.

Rothblum, E.D. (1990). Depression among lesbians: An invisible and unresearched phenomenon. *Journal of Gay and Lesbian Psychotherapy, 1(3),* 67-87.

Rothblum, E.D. (1994). Lesbians and physical appearance: Which model applies? In Greene, B. and Herek, G.M. (Eds.). *Lesbian and Gay Psychology* (pp. 84-97). Thousand Oaks: Sage Publications.

Rucker, C.E. and Cash, T.F. (1992). Body images, body-size perceptions, and eating behaviors among African-American and White college women. *International Journal of Eating Disorders, 12(3),* 291-299.

Shidlo, A. (1994). Internalized homophobia: Conceptual and empirical issues in measurement. In Greene, B. and Herek, G.M. (Eds.). *Lesbian and Gay Psychology* (pp. 176-205). Thousand Oaks: Sage Publications.

Siever, M.D. (1994). Sexual orientation and gender as factors in socioculturally acquired vulnerability to body dissatisfaction and eating disorders. *Journal of Consulting and Clinical Psychology, 62(2),* 252-260.

Striegel-Moore, R.H., Tucker, N, and Hsu, J. (1990). Body image dissatisfaction and disordered eating in lesbian college students. *International Journal of Eating Disorders, 9*(5), 493-500.

Thompson, B.W. (1994). *A Hunger So Wide and So Deep: American Women Speak Out on Eating Problems.* Minneapolis: University of Minnesota Press.

Weinberg, G. (1972). *Society and the Healthy Homosexual.* New York: St. Martin's Press.

Does Feminism Serve a Protective Function Against Eating Disorders?

Constance Guille

Joan C. Chrisler

SUMMARY. Two hundred seventeen women completed the Kinsey Sexual Orientation Scale, the Feminist Identity Scale, and three questionnaires that measured eating attitudes and behaviors. Lesbian participants were significantly more likely than heterosexual participants to work actively to improve the status of women, and they were less likely than heterosexuals to report attitudes and behaviors that are associated with eating disorders. Older women were more committed to feminist activism than younger women. Although feminist identity scores did not directly predict eating attitudes and behaviors, evidence suggests that feminism may serve a protective function against eating disorders in lesbians. *[Article copies available for a fee from The Haworth Document Delivery Service: 1-800-342-9678. E-mail address: getinfo@haworthpressinc.com]*

Feminist analyses (e.g., Brown, 1985; Chernin, 1981; Fallon, Katzman, & Wooley, 1994; Rodin, Silberstein, & Striegel-Moore, 1985; Striegel-Moore,

Constance Guille is a recent graduate of Connecticut College with a BA in Psychology. She is currently working as a research assistant in the Department of Psychiatry at Massachusetts General Hospital. This article is based on her honors thesis research.

Joan C. Chrisler is Professor of Psychology at Connecticut College. She has published extensively on feminist psychology, especially women's health, and is best known for her work on premenstrual syndrome, attitudes toward menstruation, body image, and eating disorders.

Address correspondence to: Joan C. Chrisler, PhD, Department of Psychology, Connecticut College, New London, CT 06320.

[Haworth co-indexing entry note]: "Does Feminism Serve a Protective Function Against Eating Disorders?" Guille, Constance, and Joan C. Chrisler. Co-published simultaneously in *Journal of Lesbian Studies* (The Haworth Press, Inc.) Vol. 3, No. 4, 1999, pp. 141-148; and: *Lesbians, Levis and Lipstick: The Meaning of Beauty in Our Lives* (ed: Jeanine C. Cogan and Joanie M. Erickson) The Haworth Press, Inc., 1999, pp. 141-148; and: *Lesbians, Levis and Lipstick: The Meaning of Beauty in Our Lives* (ed: Jeanine C. Cogan and Joanie M. Erickson) Harrington Park Press, an imprint of The Haworth Press, Inc., 1999, pp. 141-148. Single or multiple copies of this article are available for a fee from The Haworth Document Delivery Service [1-800-342-9678, 9:00 a.m. - 5:00 p.m. (EST). E-mail address: getinfo@haworthpressinc.com].

141

Silberstein, & Rodin, 1986; Thompson, 1994) of sociocultural factors (e.g., media messages, images of women) that influence women's body dissatisfaction have contributed greatly to our understanding of disordered eating. Cultural messages about body size, shape, and attractiveness make women feel insecure about their ability to attract romantic partners, attain glamorous jobs, or otherwise succeed in mainstream society. If women were to inoculate themselves against these messages by embracing feminism and overtly rejecting mainstream values, would they then become less susceptible to body dissatisfaction and disordered eating?

Snyder and Hasbrouck (1996) studied the relationships among feminist identity, gender stereotyped traits, and symptoms of disordered eating in 71 college students and found that body dissatisfaction and drive for thinness were positively related to passive acceptance of traditional gender roles. Individuals who scored low on measures of body dissatisfaction and drive for thinness had an active commitment to feminist values. In their survey of 3,452 women readers of *Psychology Today*, Garner and Cooke (1997) found that 55 percent identified themselves as feminists and 44 percent indicated that they held traditional values. The two groups of women differed in their degree of body dissatisfaction. Forty-nine percent of the traditional women reported that they were strongly dissatisfied and 40 percent that they were extremely dissatisfied with their bodies, whereas 32 percent of feminists were strongly dissatisfied and 24 percent were extremely dissatisfied with their bodies. Twice as many traditional women as feminist women reported that they had vomited in an attempt to control their weight. Although these numbers are unfortunately high for all women, they do suggest that feminist consciousness may help to protect women from developing eating disorders.

The results of studies of eating disorders among lesbians have been equivocal. Several researchers have found sexual orientation to be an important factor in body image. Schneider, O'Leary, and Jenkins (1993) found that lesbians were the group least concerned with physical attractiveness; heterosexual women and gay men were most concerned. The lesbian participants had a significantly higher mean body weight than the heterosexual women participants, but they expressed less concern about their weight. Lesbians indicated that they would like to lose about 8 pounds, whereas heterosexual women wanted to lose about 15 pounds. Siever (1994) also found that lesbians and heterosexual men were less dissatisfied with their bodies and less vulnerable to eating disorders than heterosexual women and gay men, both of whom placed a large emphasis on the importance of a thin body to attract sexual partners.

Other researchers (Beren, Hayden, Wilfley, & Grilo, 1996; Striegel-Moore, Tucker, & Hsu, 1990) have found similar levels of body dissatisfaction and disordered eating in lesbians and heterosexual women. Furthermore, the National Lesbian Health Care Survey (Bradford & Ryan, 1987) of 1,303 women across the United States found evidence of disordered eating. Overeating was reported much more frequently (68%) than undereating (33%) or overeating followed by vomiting (4%). Undereating was most prevalent among young lesbians (ages 17-24) and least prevalent among older lesbians (age 55+). Heffernan (1996) examined the rates of bulimia nervosa and binge eating disorder in 203 lesbians, and found that the rate of bulimia (1%) was similar to that expected among the general female population, whereas the rate of binge eating disorder (5.4%) was almost twice that previously reported in community field trials. Perhaps feminist identity is the key to understanding the conflicting results of these studies.

Lesbian culture has clearly been influenced by feminism, perhaps most importantly by cultural feminism. The messages of cultural feminism (e.g., emphasize the positive aspects of womanhood, celebrate our diversity) are embraced by many lesbians. Cultural feminism promotes social and political solidarity with other women and encourages the development of feminist identity and may then, to some degree, protect women from the attitudes and beliefs that are associated with disordered eating. Leavy and Adams (1986) found that lesbians involved in a lesbian or feminist organization, who were more removed from mainstream society, and were currently involved in a relationship had higher self-esteem and self-acceptance and more social support than those who were not. Heffernan (1996) found that increased involvement in lesbian/gay activities was associated with lower weight concerns, but that increased involvement in feminist activities was not (see Heffernan, this volume).

The purpose of the present study was to examine the relationship of feminist identity and eating attitudes and behaviors in lesbian and heterosexual women. It was hypothesized that high feminist identity would be correlated with low scores on measures of disordered eating attitudes and behaviors.

METHOD

Participants

Two hundred seventeen women participated in a study of "women and body image." The sample consisted of 52 adult lesbians (mean age 38 years, range 25-70), 56 adult heterosexuals (mean age 37 years, range 25-84), 51 young adult lesbians (mean age 20 years, range 16-24), and 58 young adult heterosexuals (mean age 19 years, range 15-24). The women were recruited from college campuses in Connecticut and the Boston area, from women's community groups and women's bookstores in Connecticut and Boston, and from lesbian support and activist groups in Connecticut, Boston, and the San

Francisco Bay area. Some college women received course credit for their participation; other participants were entered into a drawing for a gift certificate from the bookstore of their choice.

Measures

Participants completed the Kinsey Sexual Orientation Scale (Kinsey, Pomeroy, Martin, & Gebhard, 1953) and the Feminist Identity Scale (FIS; Worell & Remer, 1992). The FIS consists of 32 items that are rated on a five-point Likert-type scale and organized into four subscales: acceptance (of traditional gender roles), revelation (realization of sexism), embeddedness (immersion in female culture), and commitment (active work to improve the status of women).

Eating attitudes and behaviors were measured by three standardized questionnaires. The Eating Attitudes Test (EAT; Garner & Garfinkel, 1979) measures attitudes and behaviors that are associated with anorexia nervosa and bulimia. The Compulsive Eating Scale (CES; Dunn & Ondercin, 1981) measures food obsessions and the belief that one is unable to resist urges to eat, especially when emotional. The Three-Factor Eating Questionnaire (TFEQ; Stunkard & Messick, 1985) contains three subscales that measure dietary restraint (restriction of food intake), disinhibition (difficulty in stopping once one has started eating), and hunger.

Procedure

Each participant received a questionnaire that contained the measures described above, return envelopes, and a consent form that gave information about the study and invited the participants to enter a drawing for a gift certificate. Procedures were employed to preserve the anonymity of the participants.

RESULTS AND DISCUSSION

Weight and Height

Lesbians and Older Women Weighed More. The lesbians weighed more than the heterosexual women, $F(1, 213) = 16.76$, $p < .0001$, and the adult women weighed more than the young adults, $F(1, 213) = 14.07$, $p < .001$. The mean body mass index (BMI = weight in kilograms × height squared) for the lesbians was 26.86 (SD = 8.02) and for the heterosexuals 23.35 (SD = 4.58). The mean BMI for the adults was 26.62 (SD = 8.18) and for the young adults 23.43 (SD = 4.18). The BMI for lesbians is very similar to that reported by

Heffernan (1996), and these results support previous reports of weight differences by sexual orientation (Schneider et al., 1993) and age (Rodin et al., 1985).

Feminist Identity

Differences Based on Sexual Orientation. Lesbians scored significantly lower on acceptance of traditional gender roles and significantly higher on commitment to social change than did heterosexuals. Univariate analyses conducted on the Feminist Identity Scale (FIS) indicated that the groups differed on all four subscales: acceptance, $F(1, 213) = 18.75$, $p < .0001$; revelation, $F(1, 213) = 6.50$, $p < .01$; embeddedness, $F(1, 213) = 74.46$, $p < .0001$; and commitment, $F(1, 213) = 17.17$, $p < .0001$. Lesbians also had significantly lower scores than heterosexuals on the EAT, $F(1, 213) = 4.99$, $p < .05$, and the hunger subscale of the Three Factor Eating Questionnaire (TFEQ), $F(1, 213) = 10.55$, $p < .001$.

Age Differences. Adults were more likely than young adults to realize the effects of sexism, $F(1, 213) = 5.61$, $p < .01$. Young adult lesbians were less accepting of traditional gender roles, $F(1, 112) = 18.08$, $p < .0001$, and had lower scores on the EAT, $F(1, 106) = 5.16$, $p < .05$, and the hunger subscale, $F(1, 106) = 7.24$, $p < .01$, than young adult heterosexuals. Young adult lesbians were more committed to feminist activism than young adult heterosexuals, $F(1, 106) = 33.42$, $p < .0001$, adult lesbians (AL) were more committed than young adult lesbians, $F(1, 106) = 11.16$, $p < .01$, and adult heterosexuals were more committed than young adult heterosexuals, $F(1, 106) = 11.16$, $p < .01$.

It is not surprising that older adults are more committed to feminist activism than younger adults because age and life experience provide more opportunities to experience sexism personally. Sex discrimination, sexual harassment, and divorce are among the most common reasons that previously uncommitted women turn to feminist activism (Chrisler, 1995).

Disordered Eating

Rate of Disordered Eating. Twelve percent of the total sample scored above 30 on the EAT, which indicates clinical levels of attitudes and behaviors associated with disordered eating. Lesbians had lower clinical levels of attitudes and behaviors associated with disordered eating than heterosexuals (22% of the young adult heterosexuals, 14% of the adult heterosexuals, 8% of the adult lesbians, 4% of the young adult lesbians). Significant correlations were found among the variables for participants above (n = 26) and below (n = 191) the clinical cut-off point. For the disordered eaters, CES, r (26) = .38, $p < .05$, and disinhibition, r (26) = .44, $p < .05$, were positively correlated with revelation. For the non-disordered eaters, EAT, r (191) = .14, $p < .05$, and CES, r (191) = .16, $p < .05$, were positively correlated with revelation. EAT, r (191) = $-.15$, $p < .05$, dietary restraint, r (191) = $-.15$, $p < .05$, and disinhibition, r (191) = $-.16$, $p < .05$, were negatively correlated with commitment. Lesbians' EAT scores were correlated positively with acceptance, r (103) = .28, $p < .01$, and revelation, r (103) = .20, $p < .05$, and negatively with commitment, r (103) = $-.20$, $p < .05$. Lesbians' CES scores were correlated positively with revelation, r (103) = .20, $p < .05$, and their disinhibition scores were correlated negatively with commitment, r (103) = $-.23$, $p < .01$.

It was interesting to find that lesbians who scored higher on the Eating Attitudes Test also scored higher on the revelation subscale and lower on feminist identity scale and that Compulsive Eating Scale scores were related to revelation. These results may best be interpreted in light of Heffernan's (1996) finding that disordered eating is related to negative affect regulation in lesbians and Leavy and Adams' (1986) finding that lesbians active in lesbian or feminist organizations have better social support, self-esteem, and self-acceptance. For a lesbian to accept traditional gender roles that she does not fit is likely to arouse negative affect, as is the realization that she lives in a sexist society. Without the social, emotional, and political support provided by like-minded others involved in lesbian/gay or feminist activities, she may turn to other ways of moderating her negative emotions, such as bingeing on favorite foods.

Feminism and Disordered Eating

Standard multiple regression analyses were conducted to determine whether feminist identity predicted eating attitudes and behaviors. Acceptance of traditional gender roles was the only significant predictor, and it predicted only compulsive eating, standard beta = $-.30$, $p < .02$; less acceptance is related to more compulsive eating. There was a trend toward feminist identity as a predictor of disinhibition of eating: acceptance, standard beta = .24, $p < .06$; commitment, standard beta = $-.24$, $p < .06$. More acceptance of traditional gender roles was related to more disinhibition of eating behavior, which supports the relationship to compulsive eating. However, more commitment to feminist activism was related to less disinhibition of eating behavior, which suggests that higher levels of feminist identity/activism may reduce the risk of some disordered eating behavior.

CONCLUSIONS

Although the regression analyses did not solidly point to feminist identity as a predictor of eating attitudes and behaviors, there is evidence that commitment to feminist activism may help reduce the sense that one's eating is out of control. It may be that as women begin moving away from accepting traditional gender roles, negative emotions, such as anger, that are aroused can be coped with by binge eating. In women with more established feminist identities, this anger may be channeled into activism and thus disaggregated from eating behaviors.

Although the regression analysis did not support the theory that feminism may serve a protective function against eating disorders in lesbians, other data point to this association. Both the adult lesbian and the young adult lesbian groups scored higher on the commitment subscale and lower on the acceptance subscale and on the Eating Attitudes Test than did both the adult heterosexual and young adult heterosexual groups. Young adult heterosexual women had high scores on the Eating Attitudes Test and the lowest scores on commitment, and they also had the highest percentage of disordered eaters. This suggests that women who accepted traditional gender roles were more likely to report attitudes and behaviors associated with disordered eating.

Furthermore, when the participants who scored above the clinical cut-off on the Eating Attitudes Test were removed from the sample, significant correlations were found across all groups between high commitment scores and low Eating Attitudes Test, dietary restraint, and disinhibition scores. This suggests that women with well-developed feminist identities were less likely to restrict their food intake.

In conclusion, the answer to the question of whether feminism protected against eating disorders among lesbians in this sample will have to be "perhaps." A more accurate measurement device may shed more light on the situation. The Feminist Identity Scale is not an ideal measure of feminist identity, and it may be better suited to heterosexuals than to lesbians. This is an important area of investigation that may prove to be of considerable assistance to feminist therapists who work with women who have weight concerns. In the meantime, we can comfortably recommend that women not adopt mainstream values uncritically. Learning to accept our bodies, developing more diverse approaches to the appreciation of beauty, and heeding the messages of cultural feminism are important for promoting positive mental health among women.

REFERENCES

Beren, S.E., Hayden, H.A., Wilfley, D.E., & Grilo, C.M. (1996). The influence of sexual orientation on body dissatisfaction in adult men and women. *International Journal of Eating Disorders, 20*, 135-141.

Bradford, J., & Ryan, C. (1987). *The national lesbian health care survey.* Washington, DC: National Lesbian and Gay Health Foundation.

Brown, L.S. (1985). Women, weight, and power: Feminist theoretical and therapeutic issues. *Women & Therapy, 4(1)*, 61-71.

Chernin, K. (1981). *The obsession: Reflections on the tyranny of slenderness.* New York: Harper & Row.

Chrisler, J.C. (1995, January). My year on the NOW phone, or how I know the work of the women's movement isn't finished yet. *The Waterfall, 14(1),* p. 4.

Dunn, P.K., & Ondercin, P. (1981). Personality variables related to compulsive eating in college women. *Journal of Clinical Psychology, 37,* 43-49.

Fallon, P., Katzman, M., & Wooley, S.C. (1994). *Feminist perspectives on eating disorders.* New York: Guilford Press.

Garner, D.M., & Cooke, A.K. (1997, February). Body image survey results. *Psychology Today,* pp. 32-44, 75-84.

Garner, D.M., & Garfinkel, P. (1979). The Eating Attitudes Test: An index of the symptoms of anorexia nervosa. *Psychological Medicine, 9,* 1-7.

Heffernan, K. (1996). Eating disorders and weight concern among lesbians. *International Journal of Eating Disorders, 19,* 127-138.

Kinsey, A.C., Pomeroy, W.B., Martin, C.E., & Gebhard, P.H. (1953). *Sexual behavior in the human female.* Philadelphia: Saunders.

Leavy, R.L., & Adams, E.M. (1986). Feminism as a correlate of self-esteem, self-acceptance, and social support among lesbians. *Psychology of Women Quarterly, 10,* 321-326.

Rodin, J., Silberstein, L., & Striegel-Moore, R. (1985). Women and weight: A normative discontent. *Nebraska Symposium on Motivation, 32,* 267-307.

Schneider, J.A., O'Leary, A., & Jenkins, S.R. (1993). Gender, sexual orientation, and disordered eating. *Psychology and Health, 10,* 113-128.

Siever, M. (1994). Sexual orientation and gender as factors in socioculturally acquired vulnerability to body dissatisfaction and eating disorders. *Journal of Consulting and Clinical Psychology, 62,* 252-260.

Snyder, R., & Hasbrouck, L. (1996). Feminist identity, gender traits, and symptoms of disordered eating among college women. *Psychology of Women Quarterly, 20,* 593-598.

Striegel-Moore, R.H., Silberstein, L., & Rodin, J. (1986). Toward an understanding of the risk factors for bulimia. *American Psychologist, 41,* 246-263.

Striegel-Moore, R.H., Tucker, N., & Hsu, J. (1990). Body image dissatisfaction and disordered eating in lesbian college students. *International Journal of Eating Disorders, 9,* 493-500.

Stunkard, A.J., & Messick, S. (1985). The Three-Factor Eating Questionnaire to measure dietary restraint, disinhibition, and hunger. *Journal of Psychosomatic Research, 29,* 71-83.

Thompson, B.W. (1994). *A hunger so wide and so deep: American women speak out on eating problems.* Minneapolis: University of Minnesota Press.

Worell, J., & Remer, P. (1992). *Feminist perspectives in therapy: An empowerment model for women.* New York: Wiley.

Index

HERBS, SPICES, AND MEDICINAL PLANTS
Recent Advances in Botany, Horticulture, and Pharmacology
Edited by Lyle E. Craker and James E. Simon

Volume 1

The importance of these plants is more than economic as the scientific study of herbs, spices, and medicinal plants has made a significant contribution to the understanding of physiological processes in the biosynthesis of natural plant products and in the ecological relationships of plants within their own environment.

$95.00. hard. ISBN: 1-56022-043-0. 1986. 345 pp.

Volume 2

The book forges a link among researchers working in several disciplines associated with herbs, spices, and medicinal plants.

$95.00 hard. ISBN: 1-56022-018-X. 1987. 255 pp.

Volume 3

This volume is devoted to the review and summary of scientific information related to the botany, horticulture, and pharmacology of herbs, spices, and medicinal plants. A selected group of subject areas is presented to provide the reader with an introduction to the study of herbs, spices, and medicinal plants of the world.

$95.00. hard. ISBN: 1-56022-866-0. 1988. 205 pp.

Volume 4

This collection of articles examines the potential of natural products as pesticides, the richness of the Chinese Pharmacopeia, the similarities of Eastern Asian and Eastern North American medicinal plants, the use of borage as a source of gamma linolenic acid, and the botanical nomenclature of medicinal plants.

$95.00. hard. ISBN: 1-56022-857-1. 1989. 242 pp.

CALL OUR TOLL-FREE NUMBER: 1-800-429-6784
US & Canada only / 8am–5pm ET; Monday–Friday
Outside US/Canada: + 607-722-5857

FAX YOUR ORDER TO US: 1-800-895-0582
Outside US/Canada: + 607-771-0012

E-MAIL YOUR ORDER TO US:
getinfo@haworthpressinc.com

VISIT OUR WEB SITE AT:
http://www.haworthpressinc.com

WE'RE ONLINE!

Visit our online catalog and search for publications of interest to you by title, author, keyword, or subject! You'll find descriptions, reviews, and complete tables of contents of books and journals!

http://www.haworthpressinc.com

Order Today and Save!

TITLE	ISBN	REGULAR PRICE

- Discount available only in US, Canada, and Mexico and not available in conjunction with any other offer.
- Individual orders outside US, Canada, and Mexico must be prepaid by check, credit card, or money order.
- In Canada: Add 7% for GST after postage & handling.
- Outside USA, Canada, and Mexico: Add 20%.
- MN, NY, and OH residents: Add appropriate local sales tax.

Please complete information below or tape your business card in this area.

NAME_____

ADDRESS_____

_____

CITY_____

STATE_____ ZIP_____

COUNTRY_____

COUNTY (NY residents only) _____

TEL_____ FAX_____

E-MAIL_____
May we use your e-mail address for confirmations and other types of information?
( ) Yes ( ) No. We appreciate receiving your e-mail address and fax number. Haworth would like to e-mail or fax special discount offers to you, as a preferred customer. We will never share, rent, or exchange your e-mail address or fax number. We regard such actions as an invasion of your privacy.

POSTAGE AND HANDLING:

If your book total is:	Add
up to	$29.95	$5.00
$30.00 – $49.99	$6.00
$50.00 – $69.99	$7.00
$70.00 – $89.99	$8.00
$90.00 – $109.99	$9.00
$110.00 – $129.99	$10.00
$130.00 – $149.99	$11.00
$150.00 and up	$12.00

- US orders will be shipped via UPS; Outside US orders will be shipped via Book Printed Matter. For shipments via other delivery services, contact Haworth for details. Based on US dollars. Booksellers: Call for freight charges. • If paying in Canadian funds, please use the current exchange rate to convert total to Canadian dollars. • Payment in UNESCO coupons welcome. • Please allow 3–4 weeks for delivery after publication.
- Prices and discounts subject to change without notice. • Discount not applicable on books priced under $15.00.

❑ **BILL ME LATER** ($5 service charge will be added).
(Bill-me option is not available on orders outside US/Canada/Mexico. Service charge is waived for booksellers/wholesalers/jobbers.)

Signature_____

❑ **PAYMENT ENCLOSED** _____
(Payment must be in US or Canadian dollars by check or money order drawn on a US or Canadian bank.)

❑ **PLEASE CHARGE TO MY CREDIT CARD:**
❑ AmEx ❑ Diners Club ❑ Discover ❑ Eurocard ❑ JCB ❑ Master Card ❑ Visa

Account #_____ Exp Date _____

Signature_____

May we open a confidential credit card account for you for possible future purchases? ( ) Yes ( ) No

The Haworth Press, Inc.
10 Alice Street, Binghamton, New York 13904–1580 USA

(49) 01/00 BBC00